Tiger Woods

The Grandest Slam

TRIUMPH
BOOKS

601 South LaSalle Street
Chicago, Illinois 60605

PHOTO BY ICON SMI

Contents

Grand Finale for Woods in Masters   **5**
A moment-by-moment view of Tiger's stunning Masters Tournament.

Tiger's Tale is Better Than Fiction   **11**
The golf prodigy's story has only just begun.

Mr. Woods, Meet Mr. Jones   **13**
How does the greatest golfer of our time stack up to the legendary Bobby Jones, the greatest of his time?

A Grand Feat for Tiger Woods   **16**
Making history isn't easy—see what it took to get to the Grand Slam.

No limits on where Woods goes from here   **19**
In a year that saw Woods shatter record after record, the only question left is "What will he do next?"

Tiger Woods Player Profile   **21**
Check out all of the amazing statistics.

Ain't It Grand   **31**
Tiger proves to the world that he's in a league of his own.

Slaughter by the Sea   **38**
Tiger triumphs—and silences the naysayers—at Pebble Beach.

Young Guns   **42**
Tiger takes on Sergio Garcia in a battle of youthful stars.

The New Master   **46**
Woods made a grand showing to claim his first major title.

Members Only   **50**
Tiger secured his place among the legends of golf with the Career Grand Slam.

It's Tiger's Town   **54**
Is Tiger the greatest athlete of all time?

Tiger Woods caps "Triple Crown" with PGA Title   **56**
Woods joins the legendary Ben Hogan in the record books.

Woods Wins, Caps Sensational Summer   **62**
2000 was truly the Year of the Tiger.

In the Spotlight   **64**
Tiger is a role model for fans young and old, and he takes the job seriously.

Knock 'Em Dead, Kids   **70**
Tiger's popularity is inspiring a new generation of golfers.

Hit Me With Your Best Shot   **76**
Will the rules of the green have to change to accommodate Tiger's prowess?

Show Him the Money   **84**
Tiger's success on the green brings him plenty of green off of it.

Beware: There's a Tiger on the Loose   **92**
Can tournament organizers keep up with "Tigermania"?

Woods' Incredible Year   **96**
Tiger's ferocity left opponents and broken records in his wake.

The Grandest Slam

Grand Finale for Woods in Masters

By DOUG FERGUSON, AP Golf Writer

AUGUSTA, Ga. (AP) - Tiger Woods removed his cap and covered his face so he could flick away his tears, a rare moment when he wasn't in complete control.

"I've never had that feeling before," he said.

Professional golf hasn't seen anything like this before, either.

Slam or not, Woods was simply grand on Sunday, claiming the greatest feat in modern golf with a thrilling victory at the Masters that gave him a clean sweep of the four professional majors in a span of 294 days.

When his 18-foot birdie putt curved gently to the left and disappeared into the 18th hole, he raised his arms in triumph and almost immediately began to reflect on an achievement even he couldn't resist calling one of the greatest ever.

A runaway at the U.S. Open. History at St. Andrews. A heart-stopper in the PGA Championship. The grand finale came at Augusta National, where Woods held off David Duval and Phil Mickelson, his chief rivals, to win No. 4.

The Grandest Slam

"A Grand Slam is something we've never seen before, but we may see it before we're done."

—Butch Harmon, Woods' swing coach.

TimePix

"I have a better appreciation for winning a major championship," Woods said. "To win four of them in succession, it's hard to believe. I don't think I've ever accomplished anything this great."

Woods closed with a 4-under 68 for a two-stroke victory over Duval, thanks to a spectacular 8-iron that grazed the cup at 11th hole for a tap-in birdie and steady play down the back stretch at Augusta.

"I was so attuned to each and every shot that I focused so hard on just that one golf shot," he said. "I finally realized I had no more to play. That's it. I'm done."

Duval and Mickelson each had chances, but failed to harness the magic that has carried Woods to five of the last six majors.

Duval, believing this might be his year after three close calls, made it through Amen Corner without a mistake but took bogey on the par-3 16th, firing his tee shot over the green and missing an 8-foot putt for par.

He had two chances to catch Woods, but looked on in shock as birdie putts from 12 feet on the 17th and 5 feet on the final hole failed to fall.

Mickelson, poised to claim his first major, also missed an 8-foot par putt on the 16th hole. He also failed to cash in on birdie putts on the final two holes.

"He simply does what is required," Mickelson said.

Woods never faltered.

His lead remained at one stroke when he missed a 3-foot birdie putt on the 15th, but he traded spectacular golf for solid play with history on the line and delivered, as he has done from the time he turned pro five short years ago.

"I've succeeded in what I wanted to accomplish," Woods said as he sat in Butler's cabin waiting for last year's winner, Vijay Singh, to help him put on another green jacket. "I don't feel ecstatic yet. It hasn't sunk in."

He later took a congratulatory call from President Bush.

All that remained was what to call this remarkable feat. Purists argue that a Grand Slam is accomplished in a calendar year. Woods, emotionally drained after a relentless battle from start to finish, stayed out of the argument.

"I won four," he said with a coy smile.

Woods can simply take out his trophies from the Masters, U.S. Open, British Open and PGA Championship - and claim a place in history that no professional has occupied.

Not Jack Nicklaus, his idol, who missed his chance to hold the titles of all four majors in 1972. Not Arnold Palmer, who dreamed up the idea of a Grand Slam in 1960 but only got halfway there.

The only Grand Slam in golf not up for debate is the one that belongs to Bobby Jones, who won the U.S. Open, U.S. Amateur, British Open and British Amateur in 1930.

Fittingly, Woods finished his historic run at the tournament Jones created in 1934.

"A Grand Slam is something we've never seen before," said Butch Harmon, Woods' swing coach. "But we may see it before we're done."

Woods now has won six majors, as many as Nick Faldo and Lee Trevino

TimePix

The Grandest Slam

and only one major behind the likes of Palmer, Sam Snead and Harry Vardon. And with his winning score of 16-under 272, Woods swept the majors with a combined score of 65-under par.

The final leg at the Masters featured one dramatic moment after another involving three of the best players in the world. All of them had their chances. Every putt could have turned the tide. The crowds watched breathlessly as it all unfolded.

Mickelson shared the lead twice early in the final round, but was undone by the mistakes that cost him earlier in the tournament—a missed 2-foot putt on No. 6, a drive into the trees on No. 11 that led to bogey and left him trying to make up ground on Woods.

Still, he was only one stroke back with three holes to play when his approach into the 16th stayed on the top ridge. Mickelson aimed nearly sideways, but his ball rolled left down the slope and past the cup.

Bogey.

Duval, who wasn't even sure he could play the Masters because of an injured right wrist, three-putted for par from about 60 feet on No. 13 and can only look back at missed birdie chances on three of the last five holes.

He finished with a 67, his fourth straight year in contention at Augusta, and the first time he has ever been runner-up to Woods.

Toshi Izawa had a 67 and tied for fourth at 278, the best finish ever by a Japanese player in the Masters. He was joined by Mark Calcavecchia, who had a 72.

It was Calcavecchia who called Woods the "chosen one" after Woods completed the career Grand Slam by winning the British Open in St. Andrews last summer.

"He's not like anyone we've seen before in the game," Calcavecchia said. "It's pretty impressive."

Woods was all business from the time he arrived at Augusta National, eyes locked ahead as he walked past Nike chairman Phil Knight and an entourage of swoosh-clad executives. He and Mickelson never looked at each other on the practice green, even though they stood just 10 feet from each other.

A huge gallery that lined up outside the gates some eight hours before Woods teed off followed en masse, standing a dozen rows deep around the green as roars echoed from all corners of Augusta.

Woods punched out from behind a Georgia pine, over the first green and made bogey. Just like that, there was a four-way tie for the lead. That was only the start of an afternoon of constant momentum swings among the top players in the game.

The biggest challenge came from Duval, who had six birdies on his first eight holes and had the outright lead ever so briefly with a two-putt birdie on No. 8. His putter deserted him when it mattered the most.

"I've been here before, huh?" Duval said. "I played well today, but I had a few opportunities coming home that I wish I would have capitalized on."

Woods won his third straight tournament—so much for that "slump"—and earned $1,008,000, his second consecutive $1 million payoff.

He improved to 25-4 worldwide when leading going into the final round, and he has been particularly tough in majors. Woods now has had at least a share of the lead in 13 of the last 16 rounds of major championship golf.

He now has won 27 times on the PGA Tour in just 98 tournaments, and six majors in only 17 starts as a professional.

What's next?

Maybe a Grand Slam that no one can debate. Next stop, the U.S. Open.

"We'll find out in June," Woods said. ∎

TimePix

TIGER WOODS

Tiger's Tale is Better Than Fiction

About 15 years ago, George Plimpton wrote an article for *Sports Illustrated* that caught a nation of hopeful sports fans off guard. The story described the unbelievable exploits of Sidd Finch, a gangly Buddhist monk who had learned to utilize his exceptional mental and physical powers to throw a baseball at the unimaginable speed of 168 mph—with deadly accuracy. Sure, he'd never actually played baseball and he had some, say, offbeat tendencies (he threw with one bare foot and a single work boot rather than traditional baseball spikes), but with a little seasoning he could have become the most dominant and perhaps the most loved athlete the world had ever seen.

The fact that this April Fool's Day article was widely embraced and actually believed by many more than are willing to admit today is indicative of our greatest desire as sports fans. We are constantly, optimistically searching for that rare specimen who comes along and runs faster or jumps higher than previously imagined possible; the man or woman who emerges every generation or so and changes the very nature of their sport.

Tiger Woods was nine years old when the Sidd Finch fairy tale was concocted, but he was far from a fantasy. He had already begun to make a name for himself as a bona fide golf prodigy, and he already envisioned himself one day breaking the records of the greatest golfer before him, Jack Nicklaus.

Today, at 25, Woods has become the real-life incarnation of Sidd Finch. He routinely accomplishes feats that generations of professional golfers before him considered impossible. The world has never seen a player who can match his distance, accuracy, touch, mental toughness, or competitive drive. The manner in which he achieved the career grand slam, faster and more dominating than the four before him, instantly put him on a pedestal high above the world's best golfers of today and yesterday.

The fact that he, born to an African-American father and an Asian mother, rules a sport that for centuries was exclusive to whites is equal parts incredible and endearing. Plainly and simply, the story of Tiger Woods which, remarkably, has only just begun, could not be any more unbelievable if it had originated from the depths of the most creative imagination. ∎

Mr. Woods, Meet Mr. Jones

By JIM LITKE, AP Sports Writer

AUGUSTA, Ga. (AP) - Other golfers grow up wanting to win this tournament or that one. Tiger Woods grew up wanting to win everything.

The kid who taped a list of Jack Nicklaus' achievements to his bedroom wall and beat him to every one so far is now 25. Golf's Mozart is running out of challenges. He's already crammed a career's worth of winning into a half-dozen years on tour. He's cleared the horizon of rivals. History is the last one standing.

Counting Sunday's Masters, Woods owns six majors, as many as Lee Trevino and Nick Faldo. Ten names remain ahead of his on the list of major winners, topped by Nicklaus and the 18 titles beside his name. The earliest Woods could catch Nicklaus, assuming he wins every major staged between now and then, is at the Masters in 2004.

He needs something to aim at until then: How about Bobby Jones and a real Grand Slam?

Woods was already the youngest golfer to accomplish the career Grand Slam. Now he becomes the only one in the modern era to hold all four components of the Slam—this year's Masters, along with the U.S. Open, British Open and PGA Championship from 2000—at the same time.

Before now, golf historians argued all four majors must be won in a single year, the way Jones did it in 1930. Woods said he would let others debate the issue.

"I don't think it's right for me to comment on that," he said. "But it will probably go down as one of the top moments in our sport."

Asked what he'd say to Jones, though, Tiger had no doubts.

"First question I'd probably ask him: 'What the heck are you doing here?'"

Before the debate over a Grand Slam could begin, Woods had to win here. He began the day a stroke ahead of Phil Mickelson and three clear of David Duval. Those two were supposed to provide him with challenges for years. So far, they've barely pushed him week to week.

Mickelson has yet to win a major in 34 tries, but he began the weekend talking about this being "my time." Duval, the only player besides Woods ranked No. 1 in the last three years, was talking about this tournament being his "destiny."

They seemed on to something, though, when the three reached the back nine with Duval, playing two groups ahead, tied for the lead at 14 under, and Mickelson, playing alongside Tiger on No. 11, only a stroke behind.

That's when Tiger unleashed an 8-iron shot from 149 yards and nearly holed it. It set up a birdie and gave him back a lead he never relinquished. Woods would say later a par-saving putt from 6 feet on No. 10 was his most important shot with the short stick, and a drive at the par-5 13th that cut the corner and set up his next-to-last birdie was his best tee shot of the tournament.

So before that 8-iron gets lost among all the memorable shots from this Masters, consider: Woods needed 121 putts for the tournament, a number that ranked him 37th. And only once in the last 10 years has the Masters champion ranked lower than 13th for the week.

Woods knew he wasn't putting all that well; he got around it by simply knocking the ball closer to the hole. That's an option not available to many of his peers. It explained why more than a few gathered alongside the 18th green. They wanted to see one of golf's greatest feats themselves, even if there was no agreement on what to call it.

"The historians say you've got to win all four in one year," said Mark

TimePix

Calcavecchia, a close pal who tied for fourth. "Of course, he could still do that, too."

PGA Tour commissioner Tim Finchem noted several weeks ago there was no real authority to determine whether Woods is credited with the Grand Slam.

"I think it's a slam," Finchem said. "It's a different kind of slam than we grew up with, but different is OK."

The real reason the question matters is that Woods needs all the motivation he can get.

"I think some of the biggest accomplishments I've been privy to have been on videotape," Woods said. "I haven't been on the planet long enough to have seen the greatest athletes of all time do some of their stuff.

"I've never seen Ali fight live, and some of the stuff Michael Jordan has done has been absolutely amazing,"

Woods produces enough moments of his own to be mentioned in the same breath with Nicklaus, the best golf has ever seen. Enough to be mentioned alongside Ali and Jordan and Babe Ruth, the best from any sport.

But he needs a challenge to draw out his best, and winning the next three majors—and four in the same year—is just outrageous enough to make him do that. ■

A Grand Feat for Tiger Woods

By DOUG FERGUSON, AP Golf Writer

AUGUSTA, Ga. (AP) - Jack Nicklaus missed the cut for only the fourth time in 42 appearances at the Masters. Even rarer was what he did Sunday.

He sat in front of his television.

"I don't normally watch golf, but I watched...with great anticipation of seeing how it would unfold," he said.

While Nicklaus still has triple the number of green jackets (6-2) and major championships (18-6), Tiger Woods went 1-up on him and everyone else by winning all four majors in a span of 294 days over two incredible seasons.

TimePix

TimePix

"Is it a Grand Slam? I don't think it makes a difference," Nicklaus said. "What it's called is irrelevant. What he's done is what matters most, and what he's done is unbelievable. I call it the most remarkable feat I have ever seen or heard of in golf."

Maybe in golf.

But not for Tiger.

Winning four straight majors is every bit as awesome as Bobby Jones winning the four majors of his era in 1930. At worst, it is comparable to Byron Nelson winning 11 straight PGA Tour events in 1945 and Ben Hogan winning five of the six tournaments he played in 1953, three of them the only majors he could enter (the British Open and PGA Championship overlapped that year).

Still, Woods' greatest feat remains the U.S. Open at Pebble Beach, which started this improbable sweep of the majors.

Jones won the Grand Slam. Arnold Palmer created the professional Grand Slam. Nicklaus pursued it. Woods dreamed about it. Golf fans wondered if anyone could achieve it.

How many people truly believed a player would ever win a U.S. Open, the toughest test in golf, by 15 strokes?

The margin of victory was the largest in the 140-year history of major championships. In the modern era, the biggest blowout in a U.S. Open had come in 1970 at Hazeltine when Tony Jacklin went wire-to-wire to win by seven shots.

Woods more than doubled that margin. No one else was under par that week at Pebble Beach. He was 12 under, the first time anyone had finished double digits under par.

The feeling leaving Augusta National was not filled with as much amazement because Woods didn't do anything that wasn't expected of him, anything he had not done before.

> "What he has done, nobody has ever done. And it is unlikely that anyone will do it again."
>
> —Jack Nicklaus

True, a chance to win four straight majors doesn't come along every year. Hogan was the last man in that position, in 1954, losing the Masters in a playoff against Sam Snead.

Woods faced a similar now-or-never situation last summer at the British Open when he had a chance to become the youngest player to win the career Grand Slam. The career slam was inevitable, but this likely was his only shot to do it at St. Andrews. Woods never hit into a bunker over 72 holes and won by eight strokes.

Looking for a drama-packed final round with history on the line?

The challenge Sunday came from David Duval and Phil Mickelson, his chief rivals, with a cameo appearance by good friend Mark Calcavecchia and a disturbing lack of one by Ernie Els. Woods was never out of the lead for more than two minutes and never lost control of the tournament.

That wasn't nearly as gut-wrenching as the PGA Championship, where he had to shoot 31 on the back nine and birdie the last two holes to force a playoff with Bob May, who has as many majors as Duval and Mickelson combined.

This might not even be the greatest Masters ever. One could make a strong case for Nicklaus winning at age 46 in 1986 with a 30 on the back nine, or his incredible battle with Tom Weiskopf and Johnny Miller in 1975, or even Woods' winning by 12 shots as a 21-year-old in 1997.

Woods was more methodical than he was spectacular. He won the Masters the way Nicklaus won so many of his majors, by failing to make mistakes as his challengers stumbled.

The most memorable shot from Woods was an 8-iron from 149 on the most frightening par 4 at Augusta National that gave him a tap-in birdie.

Duval will be haunted by missing putts on the final three holes that measured a combined 25 feet. Mickelson was done in by an errant tee shot on the 11th and a three-putt on the 16th, mistakes that led to an even-par 36 on the back nine of Augusta.

The only real blemish by Woods was when he missed a 2 1/2-foot birdie putt on the par-5 15th, his fourth three-putt of the week, that extended the drama for a few extra holes.

This Masters was great for what it represented. It made Woods the first player to hold all four major championship trophies at the same time, the first to win all four in a row.

"What he has done, nobody has ever done," Nicklaus said. "And it is unlikely that anyone will do it again."

Except maybe Woods. ■

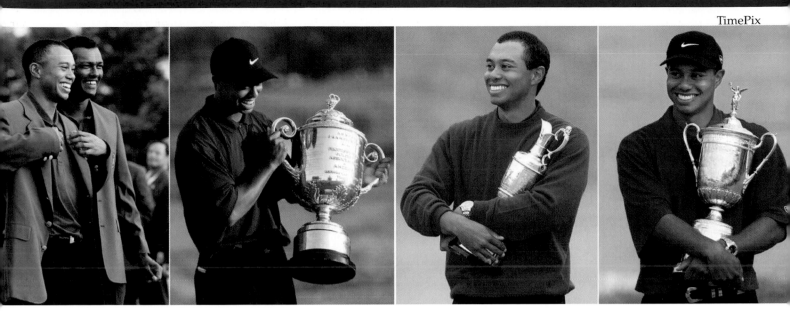

No limits on where Woods goes from here

By DOUG FERGUSON, AP Golf Writer

AUGUSTA, Ga. (AP) — Bobby Jones won the Grand Slam in 1930, was treated to a ticker-tape parade in New York, then quietly retired from golf.

Don't waste any confetti on Tiger Woods.

He's only getting started.

Still a decade away from reaching his prime, the 25-year-old Woods became the first player in modern golf to win four straight professional majors with another clutch performance in the Masters.

"I've had some special things happen to me," Woods said. "But to win four consecutive majors...I don't think I've ever accomplished anything this great."

It was only fitting that Woods claimed such an astounding feat at Augusta National, a course that Jones conceived for a tournament he created in 1934.

While Woods added his sixth major to continue a rapid pursuit of the record 18 majors won by Jack Nicklaus, his unique version of the Grand Slam was linked with Jones, who won the U.S. Open, U.S. Amateur, British Open and British Amateur in 1930.

Woods' clean sweep of the majors covered 294 days over two seasons — his 15-stroke victory in the U.S. Open at Pebble Beach in June, the British Open at St. Andrews and a thrilling playoff victory at the PGA Championship.

The remarkable journey ended at Augusta in a dramatic final round against chief rivals David Duval and Phil Mickelson, both seeking their first major.

"It's very difficult to win any of these major golf tournaments," Duval said after missing birdie chances on the final two holes to finish two strokes behind, the fourth straight year he was in contention at the Masters.

Woods now has won five of the last six majors, has been in the lead 13 of the past 16 rounds in the majors and has played the last four in 65-under par.

Whether his sweep should be considered a slam is subject to debate. Arnold Palmer, who created the idea of a professional Grand Slam in 1960, said his idea was winning them all in a calendar year. Nicklaus agrees.

Woods stayed out of the argument, noting with satisfaction that he can line up all four of the trophies on his coffee table at home.

Not long after he holed an 18-foot birdie putt on the final hole for a 4-under 68 and a four-day total of 272, talk swiftly changed from defining a Grand Slam to defining Woods.

There appears to be no limit.

Already, he has won as many majors as Nick Faldo and Lee Trevino. His next one will put him in the same group as Harry Vardon, Gene Sarazen, Sam Snead and Palmer (Jones also won seven professional majors, along with six amateur majors).

Woods is a dynasty unto himself.

In a career that began five years ago, he already has won 27 times in just 98 starts on the PGA Tour. With three more victories, he will break Nicklaus' record for the most PGA Tour wins before turning 30.

He won his sixth major in only his 17th try as a professional. Nicklaus had five majors in his 17th start.

"I don't know what you would compare it to because I'm not so sure there's something you could compare with…in modern golf," Duval said.

Indeed, Woods has been beyond compare, especially when the pressure is the greatest.

One of the most dangerous holes at Augusta is the par-4 11th, with a green that slopes toward a pond on the left. Woods choked down on an 8-iron from 149 yards and his shot grazed the cup for a tap-in birdie and a lead he never surrendered.

Clinging to a one-stroke lead over the final three holes, Woods refused to make the kind of mistake that haunted his challengers.

Duval hit a 7-iron over the green on the par-3 16th and missed an 8-foot putt for par. Mickelson, playing in the final group with Woods, left his tee shot on the top shelf of the green and missed a par putt from about the same spot as Duval.

"He simply does what is required," said Mickelson, who played Augusta's back nine in even par and finished three strokes behind.

Duval also missed birdie chances on the 17th and 18th, the last one from about 5 feet that would have tied him with Woods.

That set the stage for Woods. Once he found his drive in the fairway on No. 18, he and caddie Steve Williams slapped hands and Woods put the final touch on an incredible feat. He hit a sand wedge into 18 feet and holed the putt, raising both arms in triumph.

Exhausted from a pursuit that began in June, Woods returned to his home in Orlando, Fla., and will not play again until the Byron Nelson Classic next month.

In the meantime, he can line up the trophies from the four major championships on his coffee table before having to return the U.S. Open trophy when he defends that title at Southern Hills in Tulsa, Okla., in June.

"A Grand Slam is something we've never seen before," said Butch Harmon, his swing coach.

"But we may see it before we're done."

Jones once said of a young Nicklaus that he plays a game with which I am not familiar." No telling what he might think of Woods. ∎

Tiger Woods Player Profile

Personal Stats

Height: 6-2
Weight: 160 lbs
Born: December 30, 1975,
   Cypress, California
Year turned professional: 1996
College: Stanford University

2001 Tournament Data

Events Played: 9
Best Finish: 1st (Bay Hill Invitational,
   The Players Championship, The Masters)
Cuts Made: 9
Top 3 Finishes: 4
Top 10 Finishes: 7
Earnings: $3,392,990

Tournament Log

Date	Tournament (Tour)	Par	Round Scores	Total	Winnings	Finish
Jan. 11	Mercedes Championships (PGA)	73	70-73-68-69=280	12-under	$99,000	T8th
Jan. 25	Phoenix Open (PGA)	71	65-73-68-65=271	13-under	$152,000	T5th
Feb. 1	AT&T Pebble Beach National Pro-Am (PGA)	72	66-73-69-72=280	8-under	$68,571	T13th
Feb. 8	Buick Invitational (PGA)	72	70-67-67-67=271	17-under	$168,000	4th
Feb. 22	Nissan Open (PGA)	71	71-68-69-71=279	5-under	$58,286	T13th
Mar. 1	Dubai Desert Classic (Euro)	72	64-64-68-72=268	20-under	$129,133	T2nd
Mar. 15	Bay Hill Invitational (PGA)	72	71-67-66-69=273	15-under	$630,000	1st
Mar. 22	The Players Championship (PGA)	72	72-69-66-67=274	14-under	$1,080,000	1st
Apr. 5	The Masters (PGA)	72	70-66-68-68=272	16-under	$1,008,000	1st

DQ = Disqualified; WD = Withdraw; MC = Missed Cut

"Clearly, Tiger's the man to beat whenever he plays,
and he's creating a lot of electricity around him.
The crowds are highly charged when he's out there,
the press is highly charged, and so are his fellow players.
They're talking a lot about Tiger Woods,
and they're watching for his name on the leader boards."

Tom Watson – professional golfer

"Woods has opened the possibility that he may soon dominate his sport more completely than anybody —Nicklaus, Palmer, Tom Watson—in more than 45 years."

Thomas Boswell –
Washington Post columnist

"Tiger Woods' talent will, perforce, change the nature of the sport. I mean, look at it this way: Although Michael Jordan is far better than every other basketball player, he does not physically brutalize the game. Jordan cannot, for example, effortlessly make jump shots from center court, which is what, equivalently, Woods is capable of on a golf course."

Frank Deford – sports commentator, National Public Radio

"Woods' arsenal includes the uncanny ability to out think opponents and a cold–blooded streak, a la Nicklaus, whereby the only place is first place."

Bob Verdi – Chicago Tribune *columnist*

Ain't it Grand

A convincing British Open victory makes Tiger Woods the fifth player in history to win golf's Grand Slam

By Roland Lazenby

Ain't it Grand

Woods is the first golfer since Ben Hogan to win three majors in one year.

They came early and they stayed late. They trained harder, straining to turn their bellies flatter, their shoulders wider. To a man, it seems, the entire PGA Tour has struggled under the weight of Tiger Woods' talent. For some, like Ernie Els and David Duval, two of his closest competitors, the motivation was that same old macho thing. For others, it was the fear of more embarrassment. Regardless, they all found the same results.

They've worked to take their games to another competitive level, only to find upon arriving there, exhausted and elated, that Woods had floated away yet again, to places where they simply couldn't follow, places where no one—not even the Golden Bear, Jack Nicklaus—has been.

The blings that Woods threw off with his victory in the 129th British Open came fast and furious, with the blinding intensity of a strobe. His very best competitors may have talked of winning, but secretly, they were merely hoping to get close enough to catch a glimpse of his spectacle, to be a part of the proceedings.

Those who were so lucky had to remember

Now Woods can set his sights on the grand quest of bettering the 18 career majors won by Nicklaus, long considered the game's greatest feat. Now, though, Woods has forced the game to reconsider its hierarchy.

"He is the chosen one. He's the best player who has played the game right now," said Mark Calcavecchia. "If Jack was in his prime today, I don't think he could keep up with Tiger."

First, Woods invited such esteem with a 15-stroke victory in the U.S. Open in June, then capped the argument by taking the silver claret jug by eight strokes over Els and Thomas Bjorn. Woods stacked up the largest margin of victory in the British Open since 1913, when J.H. Taylor won by eight strokes over Ted Ray.

"The guy is simply in a different league," said Nick Faldo, who watched Woods break his British Open record set in 1990. "He is something supernatural," agreed five-time British Open winner Tom Watson. "He has raised the bar to a level that only he can jump."

In 1982, Watson won the British and U.S. Opens in the same year, a feat that Woods equalled. With his recent PGA Championship

"The guy is simply in a different league."
– NICK FALDO

to wear shades; for this special young lord was in his realm, and things were very bright as he made those giant strides across the Swilken Bridge, the youngest player ever, at 24, to complete the career Grand Slam. His par on the 18th hole at St. Andrews gave him a 69 on the day and a 19-under par to finish at 269, the lowest score in relation to par ever at a major championship.

Duval pushed to challenge on the final round, only to collapse at the end at the impossibility of it all, watching instead as Ernie Els moved ahead to secure a strange sort of record of his own —the first player to finish second in three straight majors.

But this was Woods' moment, indeed golf's moment. He became only the fifth player to win all four majors, a feat last accomplished by a 26-year-old Nicklaus at the 1966 British Open. "It's the ultimate," Woods said. "This is the home of golf. This is where you always want to win. To have a chance to complete the slam at St. Andrews is pretty special. I was able to bring it home."

victory, Woods has joined Ben Hogan as the only other player to win three majors in one year. When he accomplished that feat, it seemed like business as usual for golf's superstar. Coming into the British Open, Woods had won five official victories in a dozen events this season, the kind of numbers to crush the confidence of even his steeliest competitors.

"I need to work on my game quite a lot just to get close to him nowadays," Els had admitted a month before the British Open. Els, one of those who has dared to challenge Woods, had played well at St. Andrews over the years, almost as well as Woods himself had played the rye grass at Pebble Beach, the scene of his unprecedented 15-stroke win in the 2000 U.S. Open. Yet even with his comfort level at St. Andrews, Els couldn't raise his confidence to see past Woods.

"I have to play out of my mind," Els had said after watching Woods terrorize the tour. "My schedule is very similar to Tiger's this year," Els said. "Before his streak or before he got so ▶

Ain't it Grand

dominant, I enjoyed it. Maybe now I'll have to change my schedule. But I don't think so. I really enjoy playing with him. He's the best player in the world by far."

The only choice, Els said, is to keep chasing. Either that, or find another game. "I have to think that I can play like him," Els said, effectively summing up the challenge for every major player in the world. "If I'm dreaming, I'm dreaming."

"It's pretty phenomenal," said John Huston. "He's certainly out there in a league of his own."

An optimist could point out that the challenge presented by Woods has players across the tour pushing the grand envelope of the game, hitting the ball farther, chiseling their scores, yet finding the mental mountain they are forced to climb growing steeper with each event.

"It seems like everybody worked out harder this offseason, practiced harder, and came out more determined," said Lee Janzen. "But he's on a level that

"He's on a level that nobody can catch." — LEE JANZEN

nobody can catch."

Asked to imagine a player who could truly compete with Woods, Janzen described a golfing superhuman. "Someone who can drive the ball 300 yards every time, smart enough to play the right shots into the greens, has the imagination to curve the ball, strong enough to get out of any rough, and holes every putt in sight," he said.

That, of course, is Woods, who, like a true predator, practically sucks the brains and hearts right out of the rest of the tour. For many observers, the only real question is the egg timer on this thing. When does the awe become humorless? When is all hope extinguished? There were times at the U.S. and British Opens it certainly seemed that way. Fortunately, the answer is probably never. The money's too good, the game's too sweet, the spectacle is too much fun for fans to see any kind of slowing to the rise in popularity that Woods' performances have brought to the sport.

"Fans aren't tired of watching him," wrote Susan Fornoff of the *San Francisco Chronicle*, "as evident by the record TV ratings of his walk in the Pebble Beach park, ▶

Woods was in control from start to finish at St. Andrews.

and so the media have no cause to tire of writing about him, talking about him, and plastering his likeness all over front pages."

Besides, Woods against the rest of the golfing world isn't bad odds. He is human. He does lose on occasion. "Do we have to raise the level of our games? Absolutely," Jeff Sluman had said before the start of the Western Open in early July. "What's great about golf is we're all starting out even this week and maybe somebody can go out there and beat him. That's the challenge of this game, to try and go out there and use your 14 clubs a little better

Woods' final-round 69 gave him a total of 19-under.

than maybe he can this week."

And somebody did beat Woods in the Western. Most fans can't remember who. And that's yet another disheartening factor for the foils. Woods' play is rendering the rest of the tour virtually anonymous, even those who not so long ago seemed very capable of challenging him.

"It's not a fair comparison, comparing Tiger and me," Duval said after the U.S. Open. "He's really outplayed me for the past year." Which means Woods is cashing checks that other pros can only imagine. Woods is already the

tour's all-time leading money winner with over $16.6 million at this writing, and he's the first player to win five tournaments in consecutive seasons since Tom Watson in 1979-80. Overall, at this time Woods has 29 career victories. After the first 11 events on the PGA Tour in 2000, Woods had earned $4,949,731, an indication of just how rapidly his bank account is escalating.

At 24, he shows not even the slightest inclination to pause on his laurels for even a nanosecond. In the wake of his stupendous U.S. Open victory, the world media rolled over like a lap dog, fawning and panting. Woods wanted no part of it.

"The key is to keep trying as hard as you possibly can and not get into, I guess, the media version of trying to top this because, in essence, you really don't try and do that," he said. "You're just trying to win the tournament."

It's the old equivalent to the sports cliché of playing one game at a time. On the other hand, it goes to the heart of a basic truth about not losing focus. And if Tiger Woods is about anything, he's about focus.

"When you're out there playing, it's you against the golf course and trying to get yourself in position to win on Sunday, the back nine on Sunday in particular," Woods said. "Whoever is coming down the stretch, it doesn't really matter. You need to get there first."

Now that Woods has soared off to yet another special level, some wonder if he can stay there. It's a question that intrigues Woods himself. "I don't know if you can maintain at that level for that period of time," he said when asked if he could see playing as dominantly as he did at the U.S. Open over an extended period of time.

"But you can maintain a level probably pretty close to it. You just need to believe in your abilities, practice hard, and have things go your way." He does know this: Part of the success is the mind game, is getting the competition to believe hope is lost. "Give me a nine-, ten-shot lead every time, every single time," said Woods. "Now I realize why most of the golfers out here are balding and gray."

And so, in that sense, much of his, and the game's future, lies in the hands of those seeking to challenge him. Are they up to it? Can those bellies get any flatter? Those scores any more chiseled? To do that, they'd have to see beyond Tiger's burning strobe. And they'd have to stay close, impossible to do with each of Woods' performances pushing him so far and away. ∎

Roland Lazenby, author of numerous sports books, has won the Eckhoff Award from the National Golf Foundation for overall excellence in golf journalism.

SLAUGHTER
by the SEA

By Roland Lazenby

Tiger trounces competition at Pebble Beach

PEBBLE BEACH, California — Talk about showing 'em. The U.S. Open was supposed to be the major that Tiger Woods would never win. At least that's what the pundits said when he joined the tour in 1996. Didn't have the head. Lacked the complete game. Drives were too wild. ▶

Woods played like he had something to prove at Pebble Beach, and there were no more doubters when he was finished.

SLAUGHTER
by
the SEA

The rest of the field, as was the gallery and the millions of television viewers, was awestruck with Woods' record performance.

They ate those words in huge gulps, of course, after watching Woods blow out all of golf's circuitry with a 12-under par 272 and a 15-stroke margin over his nearest competitors at the 100th U.S. Open in June.

It was the largest margin of victory in a men's major golf championship. More important to the big picture—and a player like Woods can force an entire sport to consider the big picture—it was his third major title before he'd even turned 25. It was also the kind of performance that turned the 150 journalists on hand into an extension of the 30,000 fans on the premises and the millions watching worldwide, all focused on the game's greatest spectacle: Tiger in complete control.

> "The way I feel about my game, I just might blow everybody away this week."

They virtually stumbled after him in his final rounds at Pebble Beach, riding bikes and carts, hauling stepladders and periscopes, all eager to catch a glimpse of this eclipse of the game. "I feel like I'm running with the Spanish bulls in Pamplona, trying to keep up with the crowds following Tiger," Adam Gazal, a fan from Australia, told reporters. "It's every man and woman for themselves."

"It's mad hysteria," said Don Breen of Scottsdale, Arizona. "It's sheer bedlam."

"Tiger came here with one thing in mind: To win this tournament," said swing coach Butch Harmon, who worked with Woods. "He had a totally different mind-set from this year's Masters (a fifth-place finish), which everybody says is a course that's made for him and that he'll win a million times.

This week, the minute he left the putting green and headed for the first tee, he had a very different look in his eyes."

"You know, the way I feel about my game right now, I just might blow everybody away this week," Woods had told Harmon before the tournament. Woods then served notice with an opening-round 65, and from there the rest of the field was left to wonder how much worse it could get. The answer grew with each round.

It was the largest margin of victory in a men's major.

"Championships are supposed to identify the best golfer in the world," said Michael Bonallack, who retired in 1999 as secretary of the Royal & Ancient Golf Club after spending years setting up British Open venues. "There can't be an argument whether that was achieved this week."

Fans worldwide rushed to agree.

"Why does everybody act so crazy around him? Why can't we ever get enough? Because when we play golf, we all pretend we're him," explained Rick Crouse, a fan from California. "We all wish we could hit the ball like he does. And we all wish we could do something as spectacular as he does."

By every indication, the Open had finally, definitively established Woods as the single challenger worthy of going after the copious records of Jack Nicklaus. Few doubted that, in the process, Woods could change the very nature of the game itself.

"I'm going to try to get better," Woods said afterward. "I'm not going to win every tournament I play in, but I'm going to try."

"Having benefited for almost a decade from the dominance of a guy named Michael Jordan, I suspect we're fine for some time to come," TV executive Dick Ebersol said after witnessing the Open spectacle. "We've had two athletes in my time — Muhammad Ali and Jordan — that draw fans from outside their sport.

"Every indicator we have says Tiger is the next one." ∎

Woods rarely found trouble at Pebble, but when he did he was up to the task.

YOUNG guns

Woods holds off Garcia's charge for a hard-fought second major

By Roland Lazenby

MEDINAH, Illinois — Unlike most of his other major championships, Tiger Woods' second major, the 1999 PGA Championship, was no cakewalk, with hotshot 19-year-old Sergio Garcia, aka "El Niño," chasing him down the stretch. ▸

The battle at Medinah between young rivals Woods and Garcia was a classic, and a glorious look into the future of golf.

YOUNG guns

Entertaining the gallery with his running and skipping to celebrate each of his wildly improbable shots, Garcia made a 15-foot birdie putt on the par-3 13th to squeeze Woods on the back nine of Medinah Country Club. When Garcia finished the hole, he punched his fist in the air and shot a defiant look at Woods, who had a five-stroke lead with seven holes to play. "I wanted him to know that I was still there, and to show him that he had to finish well," said Garcia.

Given pause to think, Woods did just that, courting disaster until he regained his

it in the water' on No. 17," said Woods. "I didn't think that was fair."

Woods had taken the lead with a 15-foot birdie on the second hole and pushed it to five strokes with another birdie on the 11th. Then Garcia made his move, driving a shot right at the flag on the 219-yard 13th. The ball stopped 15 feet above the hole, setting up the huge putt.

On the 12th, Woods was chalking up his first bogey of the day by three-putting from about 60 feet. He then watched from the tee as Garcia worked the moment. "I saw him make the putt and I

"I wanted him to know that I was still there, and that he had to finish well."

Garcia wowed the gallery with his shot and reaction on 16, but in the end Tiger was too tough.

focus on the 17th for a par and the victory. He then made a two-putt on the 18th to close with an even-par 72 and a one-stroke victory over Garcia. Woods finished at 11-under 277 and won $630,000. "To come out of it on top took everything out of me," Woods admitted.

The win made Woods, 23 at the time, the youngest player since Seve Ballesteros in 1980 to claim two majors. With Garcia pushing him, there was none of Woods' trademark windmill fist pumping. Instead, he watched as the gallery got caught up in Garcia's histrionics. "I knew the crowd was changing when I heard, 'Hope you don't slice

turned away. I knew what I had to do," said Woods.

Unfortunately, all Woods could muster immediately was a double bogey. The disaster would have loomed larger except that Garcia found trouble himself, sending a drive into the trees and missing a ten-foot putt to lose par.

Then Garcia's three-wood shot off the 16th tee and left his ball resting against a tree. Instead of chipping back to the fairway, he followed his slogan, *"Suerte o Muerte"* — "luck or death." He wielded a six-iron, closed his eyes, turned his head, and fired away, then followed the shot up the fairway in a sprint, the crowd thundering with him.

His reward was a par, bagged with a two-putt from 60 feet. Woods finally owned the day, but Garcia had stolen the crowd. "I couldn't come in the clubhouse the way I wanted to," the champion lamented.

Jay Haas had a 70 and Stewart Cink a 73 that day to tie for third at 280. "I said when I turned pro that I wanted to be the No. 1 golfer in the world," said Garcia. "And so, I knew I was going to be a rival for Tiger."

"He has a tremendous amount of fight," said Woods. "You can just see it about him, the way he plays, the way he walks around the golf course, that he wants to play well. And he's going to do it at any cost. It's wonderful to see."

Despite losing all that love to Garcia, Woods had sent a message that he still ruled the golf world. It was his fourth victory in seven tournaments that year, and it was his seventh top ten finish in his first 12 majors. ■

"I saw him make the putt and I turned away. I knew what I had to do."

Tiger Woods Tiger Woods Tiger Woods Tiger Woods Tiger Woods Tiger Woods Tiger Woods

The New Master

Woods finishes a record-shattering 18-under to claim his first major title

> "I've always dreamt of playing in the Masters and winning it, and I was able to do that."
>
> — **TIGER WOODS**

AUGUSTA, Georgia — Will golf ever get over this one? Will it ever want to? Tiger Woods' first major statement to the game came at the 1997 Masters Tournament with a record 12-stroke victory that allowed him to finish at an astonishing 18-under par.

Woods' winning margin initiated what would become a familiar refrain: "the largest in any major since Tom Morris Sr. won the 1862 British Open by 13 strokes." Old Tom's record, of course, would fall when Tiger won the 2000 U.S. Open. Woods' 270 also broke the old record of 271, shared by Jack Nicklaus and Ray Floyd.

"He's out there playing another game on a golf course he is going to own for a long time,"

The New

By Roland Lazenby

said Nicklaus, who first won the Masters at 23. "I don't think I want to go back out and be 21 and compete against him."

Woods had built a nine-stroke lead through the first two rounds, then shook off some early trouble on Sunday to finish with a 3-under-par 69, good enough to collect $486,000, one of the first of many fat checks awaiting him in the coming months.

At the end of the last round, he had to close his eyes to hide tears. "My dad said last night, 'If you play well and be yourself, it would be the most rewarding round you've ever had,' " said Woods.

"I've never played an entire tournament with my A-game. This is pretty close — 63 holes.

said Kite. "He's just incredible. I don't care what his race is. He's a golfer. He's a nice person and a great kid. His parents did a helluva job raising him."

Kite said Woods "is exactly what we need in golf."

There to witness it all was Lee Elder, the first black man to play in the Masters in 1975. "This is going to bring in a nice, fresh atmosphere," he said. "I'm not saying it was a bad atmosphere before, but it's going to be better now."

At the end of the day came a phone call from President Clinton, who watched on TV. "He also said, and what meant a lot," said Tiger, "was the best shot he saw all week was the

Woods' win at Augusta earned praise from defending champion Nick Faldo, as well as from his father, Earl.

Excluding that (the front nine of the final round), I pretty much had my A-game the whole week."

"Phenomenal performance," 1996 winner Nick Faldo said. "Welcome to the green jacket."

The firsts were numerous. The first black player to win any of the four majors, the youngest Masters champion at 21 years, three months and 14 days old. Seve Ballesteros had won in 1980 at the age of 23 years and four days. Tom Kite finished second after putting up a final-round 70 to close at 282.

"To shoot 18-under on this course is incredible,"

shot of me hugging my dad."

"It was something I've always dreamt of," said Woods. "I've always dreamt of playing in the Masters and winning it. And I was able to do that."

To nail down the record, Woods faced a final two-putt at 18. "My focus never left me is what I'm trying to say," he said. "Even with the ovation I got and everybody cheering me on, it was a special moment. I knew I had to take care of business first." ■

Members Only

Woods secures his place among the legends of golf, getting there faster than anyone before him

By Larry Mayer

Dust off that chisel — it's time to add another face to the Mount Rushmore of golf. With a stirring victory at the 129th British Open Championship, Tiger Woods cemented his place among the game's immortals by becoming the fifth player in history to win the career Grand Slam. The child prodigy-turned-PGA megastar joined Gene Sarazen, Ben Hogan, Gary Player, and Jack Nicklaus as the only men to register victories in the four major championships: The Masters, the U.S. Open, the British Open, and the PGA Championship.

Even among the game's royalty, a compelling case can already be made that Woods is the most dominant golfer of all time. At 24, he is the youngest to complete the career Grand Slam. Nicklaus, the last to achieve the feat, was 26 when he did it by capturing the 1966 British Open. Player was 29, Sarazen 33, and Hogan 39.

Woods won the British Open a month after capturing the U.S. Open at Pebble Beach by a record 15 shots. It was the largest victory margin in major championship golf history, besting the 13 by Old Tom Morris in the 1862 British Open. Woods has now won 23 PGA Tour tournaments, including five majors in less than four full years as a professional. ▶

TOP PHOTOS BY AP/WIDE WORLD

Woods is the youngest player to capture golf's Grand Slam, joining (from left) Hogan, Sarazen, Player, and Nicklaus.

"If there were any two places to finish off the Grand Slam, they would be Pebble Beach and St. Andrews. It doesn't get any better than those two venues."

– TIGER WOODS

"We are seeing a guy playing at a level that we have never seen, not in my generation," said golfer Ernie Els. "He doesn't even have to be on his game and he is going to be a factor in any major in the future. When he is on, he is going to blow us all away like he did at Pebble Beach."

"Tiger will be playing blindfolded by the year 2005, at our request and at the Tour's request," said three-time British Open champ Nick Faldo. "We'll buy him a blindfold."

That might be the only way to prevent Woods from obliterating golf's record book. Winning back-to-back majors is something Nicklaus did only once during his illustrious career, when he captured The Masters and the U.S. Open in 1972. Even the Golden Bear's benchmark record of 18 major championships may be in jeopardy.

"His goals are probably to beat my goals," said Nicklaus. "I built my whole year around four tournaments. I think he's pretty much doing the same."

Woods has now won 13 events in the past 13 months. He already ranks first on the PGA Tour's career money list, having earned about $20 million. He won eight PGA Tour events in 1999, the most victories in one season since Johnny Miller also had eight in 1974. Woods has won nine times this year and has finished in the top five in 14 of 17 PGA Tour tournaments. Nicklaus never won more than seven events in a year.

"I had my stretches where I played well, where I never finished out of the top ten," said Nicklaus. "But with today's number of good players, I think it's probably more astounding than my record was. He's done it every time he's played."

A further comparison of Woods and Nicklaus reveals that Tiger is at least on pace to supplant the Golden Bear as the greatest golfer of all time. At the age of 24, Nicklaus had won three majors to Tiger's five, while Woods leads in victories, 21-12. It should be noted that Woods turned pro at 19, while Nicklaus was 21. In their first 71 PGA Tour events, Tiger won 16 times and Jack was victorious on 10 occasions.

While Nicklaus idolized Bobby Jones, Tiger modeled himself after Nicklaus. As a kid, Woods pasted a newspaper article listing a few of Nicklaus' accomplishments on his bedroom wall. These days the two often engage in friendly conversation.

"He sees a lot of himself in me," said Tiger, "the way we play the game, the concentration level. It's funny, we can't stop talking. He always wants to share with me. I love it. Here's the greatest of all time and he wants to give me knowledge. It's a very unique bond."

Fittingly, Woods completed his career Grand Slam at historic St. Andrews, Scotland, which is considered the most famous golf course in the world.

"If there were any two places to finish off the Grand Slam, they would be Pebble Beach and St. Andrews," said Woods. "It doesn't get any better than those two venues. St. Andrews is very special; it's the birthplace of golf. I have the greatest admiration for this course, the conditions and traditions this golf course has, and the history behind it."

Woods first competed in the British Open in 1995, the last time the tournament was held at St. Andrews. Then an amateur, he finished tied for 68th. Now, as a winner of the career Grand Slam, Woods is in select company, to say the least.

Nicklaus won 70 PGA Tour tournaments and was the leading money winner eight times. Sarazen (1902—1999), the first Grand Slam winner, captured seven majors including three PGA Championships, two U.S. Opens, one Masters, and one British Open. He won 38 tournaments on the PGA Tour and hit the most famous shot in golf history, a double eagle in the 1935 Masters.

Hogan (1912—1997) won 68 pro tournaments, including 13 in 1946 and 10 in 1948. He won nine majors including four U.S. Opens, two PGAs, two Masters, and one British Open. He was nearly killed in a car accident in 1949, but valiantly returned to play championship golf. He suffered a broken ankle, broken ribs, a double fracture of the pelvis, and massive internal injuries. Doctors performed emergency surgery when blood clots formed in his legs, and they feared he would never walk again. Hogan was walking in three months and back on the Tour the following year.

Player, voted the top athlete in the history of South Africa, won 21 PGA Tour events and nine majors including three Masters, three British Opens, two PGAs, and one U.S. Open. ∎

IT'S TIGER'S TOWN

A case can be made for Woods as the most dominant athlete of all time

By Aaron George

Babe Ruth. Michael Jordan. Muhammad Ali. Jim Brown. Wayne Gretzky.

By now, even the most stubborn Tiger detractors have seen enough to grant Woods his rightful place among this legendary class of athletes. But astute observers of the ever-improving, 25-year-old phenom can make a strong case for something still more startling: Tiger Woods is, or will go down as, the most dominant athlete of all time—any sport, any era.

Powerful words, but when you consider the subject at hand, nothing in our lexicon can overstate his stranglehold on the sports world. His victories at Pebble Beach and St. Andrews this year, giving him the the fifth and fastest career grand slam in history, have all but secured his place atop the golf world, past and present. And when you compare his dominance in golf to that of the aforementioned greats in their sports, Tiger tames them all.

Ruth was undoubtedly the most prolific slugger of his time, and he played for a team that dominated its era. But he also had the support (and hitting protection) of an armful of Hall of Fame teammates, not to mention the hitter-friendly dimensions down the lines at Yankee Stadium. Woods, on the other hand, is rewriting the record books with no one but a caddie in his corner, a field of the world's best players gunning for him every week, and courses that the PGA continuously tries to Tiger-proof to create a more even playing field.

Jordan, widely recognized as the best basketball player ever to don a jersey, didn't win a championship until his seventh season in the NBA, at the age of 28. Woods, conversely, won the Masters in only his first full year as a pro in 1997. That was when he rag-dolled a field of the world's best golfers, cruising to an unheard-of 18 under par and raking in $486,000 for one weekend of play at just 21 years of age.

Muhammad Ali

Wayne Gretzky

Neither can Ali match Woods' level of dominance. Although he may have been "The Greatest" boxer ever, Ali will forever be noted alongside rivals like Sonny Liston, Joe Frazier, and George Foreman. When history recognizes the giants of golf, Tiger Woods quite likely will stand alone.

Brown, like Ali, is regarded by many as the best of all time in his sport. But the gridiron legend may trail Tiger when fans and writers ponder the greatest athlete ever. While Brown's rushing-yardage record was surpassed 16 years ago, Woods is accomplishing things on the golf course that the sport has never seen in more than a century of competitive play.

Gretzky exploded onto the professional hockey scene similar to the way Woods has captivated the golf community, and he maintained a level of dominance throughout most of his career. But critics often called him one-dimensional, and, unlike Jordan, he left the game well after his superstar skills had begun to diminish.

One can only imagine the things Woods will achieve if he plays professional golf into his 40s and 50s, if not longer. And one can only imagine if another like him, in any sport, will come along again. ∎

Michael Jordan

Jim Brown

Babe Ruth

55

Tiger Woods caps "Triple Crown" with PGA title

By Jimmy Burch

LOUISVILLE, Kentucky — Move over, Ben. You've got company. Tiger Woods is in the house, and he's here to stay.

Woods, a playoff winner Sunday in the PGA Championship at Valhalla Golf Club, joined Fort Worth legend Ben Hogan as the only professional golfers to win three major championshps in one season.

Woods completed his version of the "Triple Crown" by holding off Bob May with a birdie and two pars in a three-hole, aggregate playoff. Woods forced the playoff by burying a five-foot birdie putt on the final hole of regulation to join May as the only golfers in history to reach 18-under par at the PGA.

For Woods, it marked his third consecutive victory in a major championship and the third consecutive time he has recorded a tournament scoring record on the way to hoisting the hardware. Woods, who closed with a 67, posted sub-par scores in his final 14 rounds at major championships this season, with a scoring average of 67.7 during that stretch.

"That is dominant," said Tom Watson, who finished in a tie for ninth at the PGA. "Tiger is doing things nobody else has ever done. You are seeing a phenomenon that the game

AP/Wide World

may never, ever see again." Indeed, none of Hogan's victories during his 1953 "Triple Crown" included a 72-hole score lower than 274—four strokes higher than Woods' total Sunday. But the fact that Hogan won five times in six starts, including a three-for-three sweep in 1953 majors (he skipped the PGA), has caused some veteran observers to wonder if Hogan hasn't been swept aside in a rush to esteem Woods.

"People forget that Hogan did this, too. And that year might have been even better than Tiger's year," said Dave Anderson, 71, a columnist for the *New York Times*.

Dan Jenkins, renowned author and golf writer from Fort Worth who covered Hogan in his prime, said he places the two seasons on "equal footing." The merits of both accomplishments may be debated, said Jenkins, but there's no question Woods' 2000 season and Hogan's 1953 campaign constitute two of the four greatest years

AP/Wide World

ever turned in by a golfer. The other candidates would be Bobby Jones' "Grand Slam" in 1930 (two professional and two amateur majors) and Byron Nelson's 11 straight victories in 1945.

"It's a toss-up between those four, depending on your perspective," said Jenkins, 70. "But what Tiger did is definitely one of the greatest four years in golf history."

Woods achieved his defining moment by shaking May, a career non-winner on the PGA Tour, with a 20-foot birdie putt on the first hole of the aggregate playoff. When he added two additional pars and May could not answer with a birdie, Woods won for the fourth time in the past five majors contested on the PGA Tour.

This victory, he said, was his sweetest in a major because May—who closed with a 66—made the chase extremely difficult.

"It was one memorable battle and I really enjoyed it," Woods said. "We never backed off from each other. It was birdie-for-birdie, shot-for-shot . . . That's as good as it gets, right there."

Indeed, the closing round included more plot twists than a Stephen King novel. May, 31, took the lead on the second hole with a birdie-bogey swing and never relinquished it during regulation. At the 72nd hole, May drained a 15-foot birdie putt from the fringe that forced Woods to answer with a birdie of his own to continue his historic quest.

Despite falling a stroke short, May said the fact that he strung together three consecutive 66s at Valhalla should prove "there was no fluke" about his presence in a final-round pairing at a major championship.

Woods said joining Hogan as a "Triple Crown" winner made for "a special day."

"I have a lot of admiration for a lot of great champions that have played the game," Woods said. "Ben Hogan won so many tournaments, it's scary. He was incredible. He played at a level that not too many players could ever attain."

But Woods has attained that level three times this season. In February, he became the first golfer since Hogan in 1948 to win six consecutive PGA Tour events. Last month, Woods joined Hogan, Jack Nicklaus, Gary Player, and Gene Sarazen as the only golfers to complete the career grand slam. Now, Woods and Hogan are the only professional golfers with "Triple Crown" seasons.

In one regard, Jenkins said Woods has eclipsed Hogan.

"I never thought I'd live to see the day that a golfer would be the world's most famous athlete," Jenkins said. "But I have. It's incredible."

Incredible, of course, could also serve as an appropriate summation for Woods' 2000 season. Or Hogan's, in 1953.

AP/Wide World

Woods wins,
caps sensational summer

Staff and Wire Reports

More than 50,000 people came out to watch Tiger Woods win the Canadian Open. As usual, he gave them much more—another remarkable round, another shot they will never forget.

Pushed to the limit by an unlikely challenger, Woods found another way to build upon his legend by wrapping up his ninth victory of the year with a six-iron from 218 yards—out of a bunker, over the water, right at the flag—that sealed his one-stroke victory against Grant Waite.

So ended perhaps the greatest summer in golf.

Woods won five of his seven tournaments. Three were major championships, including one that completed the Grand Slam. All five included scoring records. All five were filled with amazing shots that only Woods has in his repertoire.

"He's an extraordinary player who comes along once every generation —or in his case, maybe once in forever," said Waite, who matched Woods shot for shot except for the one that left the 36-year-old from New Zealand shaking his head.

Clinging to a one-stroke lead on the par-5 18th, Woods blasted out of the bunker down the right side of the fairway and the ball took its familiar flight—crisp and high, lost among the gray clouds spitting rain, descending as the record crowd roared with anticipation, then landing about 18 feet behind the hole in the first cut of rough.

"When pressure is at its peak, that's when your concentration level is at its highest," Woods said. "It builds to a crescendo."

Waite, whose only PGA Tour victory was in 1993, did his part. He hit a 5-iron into 20 feet for a chance at eagle, and forced Woods to go for the green instead of laying up. Waite's putt slid by on the right, and Woods chipped down to a foot and tapped in for birdie, closing out a 7-under-par 65 and yet another championship.

"I've had a wonderful summer," Woods said.

He has won 9 of 17 tour events this year, including 3 in a row. And he has set scoring records in his past five victories—12 under at the U.S. Open, 19 under at the British Open,

18 under at the PGA Championship, a 21-under 259 at Firestone.

Woods was 22 under for his final 49 holes and finished at 266, the lowest 72-hole score in the 22 years that the Canadian Open has been played at Glen Abbey Golf Club in Oakville, Ontario.

Woods' nine are the most PGA Tour victories in one year since Sam Snead won 11 times in 1950. He earned $594,000, giving him more money in his past 38 tournaments— $14.9 million—than anyone else in their career.

And Woods can now add the Triple Crown to the Grand Slam he completed by winning the British Open at St. Andrews. He became the only other player besides Lee Trevino in 1971 to win the U.S. Open, British Open, and Canadian Open in the same year.

Brandt Jobe of Southlake and Paul Stankowski of Flower Mound both shot 71 and finished at 277.

© 2000, *Fort Worth Star-Telegram.*

AP/Wide World

IN THE SPOTLIGHT

Tiger Woods is honored to be a role model for fans young and old.

By James Raia

Charles Barkley, the NBA's resident philosopher, disdains the label "role model." Several years ago, he declared, "I am not a role model." He had his reasons.

But there are professional athletes—such as Grant Hill, Steve Young, and Cal Ripken Jr.—who welcome, even embrace, the responsibilities that come with being revered by fans.

For pro golfer Tiger Woods, being a role model is an honor and a situation he relishes. Not only can he enlighten children, but he is widening the scope of his sport's popularity.

"I'm in a position where I can influence kids' lives in a positive way," Woods said recently. "All these years kids have been told that there's only a certain amount of core sports in America—basketball, football, golf, track, baseball. They're taught those are our sports in America and those are the only things we can play.

"Inner-city kids are trained to believe that. I'm saying, 'Hey, guys, there's another sport out here. It's called golf, and I want to make this available to you. I want to make you interested.'"

Woods takes his beliefs to the golf course. He gives youth clinics around the country, promoting

**For Tiger Woods, giving interviews and
signing autographs for fans are just part of the job.**

the game and instilling the value of good sportsmanship. Also, through the Tiger Woods Foundation, he is creating other opportunities for underprivileged young people.

So far, the combination of Woods' gold tournament success and his role model status could not have grown any faster. Children and their parents are listening to his message. People who had limited understanding of such golf terminology as eagle, birdie, par, and bogey are now taking to the links. At the very least, they are tuning in and watching television when Woods takes to the golf course.

"Golf has shied away from racism for too long," Woods recently told a reporter for Time magazine. "Some [country] clubs have brought in tokens [non-white players], but nothing has really changed. I hope what I'm doing can change that."

But the ripple effect, or "Tiger Striping" as it has been called by one Woods watcher, transcends racial, social, cultural, and athletic barriers.

"He is absolutely not bigger than golf," explained Tiger's father and mentor, Earl Woods. "And he will never be bigger than golf. But he will transcend golf in that he will venture outside its boundaries and

Tiger Woods
received a warm
welcome in Thailand,
his mother's
native country.

make contributions (to society). But to say Tiger is bigger than golf, no. No one person is bigger than the sport than they play."

While Woods' increasing influence has enveloped golf, it has also garnered the attention of academics. His status as a role model—a controversial topic in these days of escalating sports salaries and athletes' erratic behavior—has been accepted and encouraged en masse. Educators, social commentators, fellow athletes, and Tiger-watchers in all walks of life all have positive opinions on the subject.

"It would seem there has been a break-through, and Woods is at the forefront," Norman Baker, an associate professor of

history at State University of New York at Buffalo, told Golf magazine. "He is seen as articulate and representative of the gentlemanly qualities of golf.

"This isn't some guy who showboats. He is the modern-day Jackie Robinson. If you hand-picked someone to break barriers, if you created a model, Tiger Woods fits."

Sports psychology expert Rick Wolff groups Woods with such athletes as David Robinson, Hill, Ripken, and Young. All share similar beliefs about their responsibilities as public figures and role models.

"Most of the guys who tend to share the same sentiments on and off the play-ing field do like being role models," said

Wolff, the editor at Time-Life Books who is coordinating two upcoming books on Woods. "They embrace it. These are the guys who say, 'Yes, we want the next generation to look up to us.'"

In Woods' case, the role model situation makes perfect sense to Wolff.

"Tiger is a bright, affable young guy who does seem to enjoy himself," Wolff said. "He seems to have an idea of where he's going and where's he's been. He truly does not seem to have any out-ward problems with the expectations and pressures that he's pretty much put upon himself, which is good. But he's also someone who has developed a pas-sion for the sport he plays and enjoys the challenge."

Tiger Woods on "The Oprah Winfrey Show" — April 1997

From a golfing perspective, Houston teaching pro Butch Harmon, who began working with Woods four years ago, believes Woods' appeal is simple. He's genuine. The throngs who are listening to Woods, Harmon says, don't hear bravado or see the bizarre.

And, as Woods has said about himself, "whatever you see in front of you, that's what you've got."

"First of all, he's still a kid," said Harmon, whose list of clients includes Greg Norman. "People love that, to see a younger person succeed in a man's world, so to speak. And that smile. You've got to love it. It's genuine. It's not a put-on thing. It's Tiger. If you're around him a lot, he's always laughing at you and smiling. He's really enjoying himself out there."

From an athlete's perspective, whatever professional jealousies might have arisen, they seem to have been overshadowed by endearment. To borrow from a catchy,

old advertising jingle from a well-known frozen cake company, "Nobody doesn't like Tiger Woods."

Consider, as one example, the opinion of Mike Schmidt, the retired Hall of Fame third baseman.

"I'm tremendously impressed by Tiger Woods, as I'm sure everybody is. But for me mostly it's because in a day and age where most of the young up-and-coming stars in sports kind of rub me the wrong way at times with their style and the image they project to kids and fans . . . Tiger is a breath of fresh air.

"He's a polished kid who's willing to stand up and say 'I'm thankful for where I am and what God has allowed me to do. And for that I'm going to be a role model. It's as important for me to influence young kids in new directions as it is to win golf tournaments.'

"I truly believe that he believes he's on some sort of mission. To me, that's very impressive for a young man to not only

accept the pressures of winning golf tournaments, but to understand and accept all the pressures that society is going to put on him for obvious reasons."

As much as anyone, however, Woods knows his image and his role as a model citizen. He knows that he left Stanford University after two years, and he knows he has promised to complete his studies and earn a degree. He knows that children admire him and listen to every word he says.

He also knows how to seek help from Michael Jordan, Phil Knight, or a host of others in any field of expertise imaginable.

Woods also chooses to reflect upon his upbringing when he considers his ever-increasing public stature.

"My parents wouldn't let me practice until I had my homework done – all the way up until I entered high school. That was just the law," Woods recalled. "Of course, I fought it growing up. But now I'm still thankful that they did that." ■

AP / WIDE WORLD PHOTOS (3)

"If you are ever given the chance to be a role model, I think you should always take it because you can influence a person's life in a positive light, and that's what I want to do. That's what it's all about."

Tiger Woods

KNOCK'EM DEAD, KIDS

Tiger Woods' popularity is prompting an unprecedented number of young people to pick up golf clubs for the first time.

By James Raia

STEVE LEVIN / ACTIVE IMAGES

Tiger Woods: An inspiration for many young people

Don Deavens is a custom golf club builder in Sacramento, California. He owns a small company located in a warehouse that's surrounded by barren agricultural fields, a lower middle-class sub-division, and Arco Arena, the playing facility of the NBA's Sacramento Kings. There also happens to be a driving range in the neighborhood.

Two years ago, Deavens had had enough of the real estate business. He had a love for the game of golf, so he "decided to try and make a living at it" and opened his own business.

Small business owners often have enough to worry about, but one new component in the world of making and selling golf clubs has arrived unexpectedly for the new entrepreneur. And although it's hardly profitable, it's just fine with Deavens.

With increasing frequency, Deavens sees young boys—golf bags and clubs slung over their shoulders—walking from their homes after school to the driving range.

"It's a good mile or so," Deavens said. "But these kids, obviously influenced by Tiger Woods, are out there. They have old bags and clubs bigger than they are."

On one recent occasion, one of the boys heading to the driving range walked into Deavens' Tru-Flite Golf Company and asked, "Hey, how much are your drivers? My birthday is coming up and my mom's going to give me $80. Will $80 buy a driver?"

The youngster's current "set," according to Deavens, consisted of about a half-dozen irons and woods, all too big, some cracked, some rusty.

"He had old persimmon woods, rusty blades and shafts," Deavens recalled. "He must have walked at least a mile or 1½ miles. I see a steady stream of young kids walking down the street walking down to the driving range with their bags on their backs. It's really incredible to see.

"It made me think back to when I was a kid hanging

around the schoolyard playing basketball. Now kids are doing the same thing with their golf clubs. I think it's absolutely incredible."

Deavens didn't sell the boy a driver, but instead asked the youngster if he could look at his clubs. He recalled that the boy, about nine or ten years old, had a 43-inch driver.

"Obviously, the clubs were way too big for him, but he said, 'I can hit this driver 150 yards,'" Deavens explained. "Well, I told the boy I would cut all his clubs down for him."

Suffice it to say, he did it for no charge.

There's no proof, but chances are that Deavens' tale is representative of Tiger Woods' growing influence on children, particularly minority children, throughout the United States and elsewhere. Driving ranges are packed until sundown. Tee times are more difficult to acquire. Competition between courses has become intense. Courses are now no longer just marketing women's days, but kids' days and family days, too.

"I don't think there's any doubt that Tiger Woods is having an impact," said Bill Burbaum, vice president of communications for the National Golf Foundation in Jupiter, Florida, which tracks trends in the sport, "but I don't think people are just rushing out there. But there may be a certain percentage of the population that's saying, 'Hey, listen, I've been thinking [about golf] and now I'm going to give it a whirl.'

"How many dads out there were trying to get their kids to go and play golf and the kid said, 'No, I want to play field hockey or skateboard' or whatever. Are those kids now saying, 'Hey, dad, sure, I'll go out there with you.' There's all this enthusiasm. But now we have to know if the other things, availability of tee times, lack of intimidation, all those things are in place, to allow the new player to go there and experience the game without having a terrible experience."

In a recent business piece on CNN entitled "Tiger Mania," the global news network said that an estimated 1 million people would take up golf

Tiger's younger fans show their support during the U.S. Open in June.

ABOVE: Tiger Woods helps a girl with some fundamentals during a Tiger Woods Foundation Junior Golf Clinic on June 16, 1997, on Randall's Island in New York. BELOW: Tiger helps a Texas youngster with his swing during another clinic on May 11,1997.

this year in the United States. The story credited the phenomenal growth of golf to Tiger Woods' recent success.

Woods, of course, has established his own foundation to teach golf to inner-city children. The United States Golf Association also established a new inner-city youth golf program. Its promotion for the program includes a national television commercial featuring a subject not too different from that of the boys who walk to the driving range in the farmlands of Sacramento. It shows inner-city boys carrying their clubs on the train out of the city and onto driving ranges in the country.

"Time is only going to tell what influence Tiger Woods is going to have [on golf]," Burbaum said. "We do not have any statistics that will tell you that in the month of May or June golf participation jumped a certain number of points.

"What I can tell you is that since the Masters [a tournament Tiger Woods won easily] we've gotten a lot of calls from people saying, 'We're seeing a lot going on in our area, what' s going on nationally?' We won't have specific numbers for a year or so, but what we have seen is a lot of enthusiasm."

Despite a lack of time to decipher Woods' influence with statistics or charts and graphs, Burbaum believes more children and more adults—and often families together—are taking up the game in record numbers. The trend, he said, began before Woods turned professional. The young champion, however, has since prompted more competition among manufacturers, courses, apparel lines—any component of the game of golf.

In short, the business of golf is booming.

"What it has also come down to is that golf has become part of the corporate fabric of America," Burbaum said. "How many business meetings, how many sales conferences, how many annual meetings are built around golf? It just suits the young man or woman."

Although public courses may no longer be able to offer weekend tee times because of crowded facilities, new golfers are no longer as intimidated as they once were to start playing. Many short-distance or "executive" par-3 courses are being established, and courses have become creative, offering ways to encourage the new player.

"Tiger Woods is a godsend to golf and to those people in the business of golf," Burbaum said. "The X generation was already beginning to accept golf; it was no longer the old fuddy-duddy's game. John Daly sort of softened up the beachhead for that. He was the every-man guy.

"But can you say that John Daly really had an impact on golf participation in the United States? I'm not so sure he did. The last time anyone really credited one golfer with an increase in golf participation in the United States was Arnold Palmer back in the 1960s. And at that time Arnold Palmer and television were the magic potion. I don't think Arnold Palmer would have been as big if it weren't for television," he said.

"But now, with Tiger Woods, you've got a charismatic player, a role model, whatever he is, who has burst upon the scene when the younger generation, today's generation, was already beginning to look at the game of golf differently." ■

Tiger watches the flight of 11-year-old Kousuke Onuma's ball during a clinic at the Tiger Woods Invitational in Hanno, Japan.

Tiger shows an overflow crowd how it's done at his youth clinic, held during the Tiger Woods Invitational in Hanno, Japan.

"I think Tiger is a great addition to the game of golf."

Tour professional Greg Norman

HIT ME WITH YOUR BEST SHOT

Tiger Woods' success shouldn't force big changes in how golf courses and equipment are designed, experts say.

BY JAMES RAIA

It is no longer surprising when Tiger Woods is mentioned in the same breath with legendary golf names like Jones, Nicklaus, Palmer, and Nelson.

Nevertheless, when at 21 you've been compared to athletes like George Mikan, Wilt Chamberlain, Lew Alcindor, and Bobby Hull, it raises some questions.

What could be at stake, if you believe some golf players and fans, is that Woods' dominance could force major changes in the sport, from club and ball restrictions to course alterations.

The United States Golf Association (USGA)—which, along with the Royal and Ancient Golf Club in St. Andrews, Scotland, has determined the rules of golf since 1952—has heard such concerns, and this isn't the first time.

If such drastic measures sound unlikely, consider the aforementioned athletes. Hockey, basketball and others have undergone major and minor changes because of superstars' mastery of their respective sports.

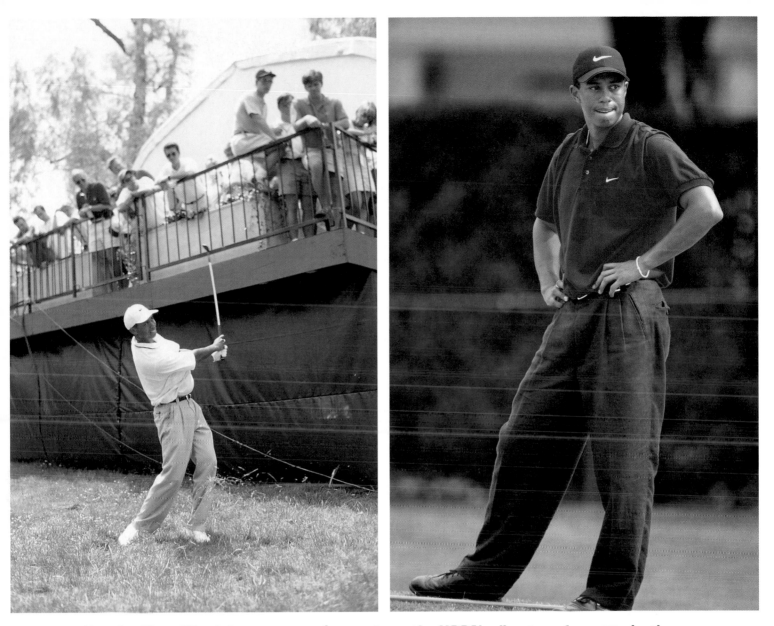

Despite Tiger Woods' success on the pro tour, the USGA's director of communications insists that "you don't change the game for one person."

Mikan was basketball's dominating center in the 1940s and 1950s. Because he was so imposing, the NBA widened the lane to the basket from 6 to 12 feet and even briefly (for one game) raised the basket to 12 feet. A decade later, Wilt Chamberlain's presence resulted in another 4-foot widening of the lane.

And, before he converted to Islam and changed his name to Kareem Abdul-Jabbar, Alcindor's dunking abilities at UCLA prompted the NCAA to ban the dunk for several years.

Hockey superstar Hull whipped his slap shot so powerfully from his bent "banana blade" hockey stick that the NHL restricted the curve allowance on his stick to 1.5 inches. The league has since reduced the curve angle twice to its current half-inch standard.

In addition, in Major League Baseball, the four-some of Denny McLain, Luis Tiant, Don Drysdale, and Bob Gibson overwhelmed batters so completely in 1968 that the pitching mound's apex was lowered from 15 to 10 inches and the strike zone was narrowed.

But what of Woods, who won 7 of his first 22 pro tournaments (6 of them PGA events) and was in 2000 primed to become the first PGA player to win $2 million in official tournament prize money in one season?

Tiger Woods chips out of a
bunker during play at the
1997 U.S. Open.

JAMIE SQUIRE / ALLSPORT USA

Do his 320-plus yard drives, which dominate tour statistics, warrant the alteration of some of the historic courses around the country? Should the caretakers of the prized layouts around the courses build more fairway traps, as some have suggested? And are there other ways being considered to curtail Woods if he continues to storm through his first full season as a professional?

"You don't change the game for one person," said Marty Parkes, the USGA's director of communications. "When Wilt Chamberlain scored 100 points in a game, they didn't raise the rim, did they?"

While other sports, mostly in bygone eras, made changes, golf faces two concerns if it decides to try to slow Woods down. First, many of the courses used on the PGA Tour lack space to expand. And, even if space wasn't a concern, wouldn't expanding make it more difficult for other golfers, too?

Besides, on par-5 holes, more length actually could give Woods an advantage. While he could still reach some holes on his second shot, more players would no longer be able to do it.

ABOVE: Tiger blasts out of the bunker on the second hole during the third round of the 1997 U.S. Open.
BELOW: On the green with Nick Faldo during the final round.

TOP: AP / WIDE WORLD PHOTOS; BOTTOM: DOUG PENSINGER / ALLSPORT USA

"We've kind of been down this road before," Parkes said. "People sometimes forget that. When the newest player comes up, they think this has never happened or is unprecedented. But in a lot of cases it's not really unprecedented."

Woods has already realized the irony of his success.

"I think that's fine," he said about potential course changes prompted by his success. "If they are going to make it harder on me, they're going to make it harder on everyone else, too."

Some of his competitors have apparently given the matter some thought. Jesper Parnevik, the young Swede who held a first-round lead at the Masters, only half-jokingly suggested that courses create "Tiger Tees" 50 yards farther back from the tees the other pros use. Bernhard Langer is partial to the idea of installing more "Tiger Bunkers" farther into holes.

The USGA and its European counterpart meet once a year to discuss the rules of golf. Changes, updates, revisions, and clarifications to the game are made every four years, the last time in 1996, according to the USGA.

ABOVE AND RIGHT: Tiger Woods had an atypically poor showing at the Memorial Tournament in Dublin, Ohio, in June. He finished in a tie for 67th place.

In the intervening four-year periods, the USGA fields thousands of inquiries about the rules of golf. These requests for rule interpretations—from amateurs and pros alike—ultimately prompt discussions about specific rule adjustments or revisions.

"If you completely set a course for one person, you're putting 155 other people at a disadvantage," said a USGA spokesperson who requested anonymity. "As far as our policies go, we set the policies up not for one person, but for the field. . . . As far as the USGA championships he (Woods) has

played in, changes haven't been a consideration.

"No one has said, 'Do we set this up because there's a couple of people in field who hit the ball a long way?' We take the course and we set it up so that it will play at its best as a tournament championship course.

"We don't always go to the very back of a par-3. We don't want all the par-3 holes playing the same distance. You want to vary a two- or a one-iron on one hole, a four-iron on another or a seven-iron or a wedge on another. There's not one individual who's

going to affect the setup of a course as much as it is that we want to set up the course so that it tests the player, all the players, as best it can."

While Woods' ascension is unlike that of any other golfer in history, he isn't the first player whose skill had the game's guardians answering questions about the rule changes. When Bobby Jones reigned the tour and overwhelmed fields en route to the Grand Slam in 1930, there were rumblings about the game. Similar thoughts arose when Byron Nelson won 11 straight

tournaments in 1945 and Jack Nicklaus raced to a nine-stroke victory at the 1965 Masters.

"When Jack Nicklaus came on (the tour), he was hitting the ball tremendous distances," Parkes said. "You forget about that now because he's been around for so long and he's getting older and he doesn't hit it as far.

"If you go back and read the press in those days, in the mid-1960s, a lot of people were saying the same thing—that Jack Nicklaus was going to make all these golf courses obsolete and what are we going to do. We all know now that he's the greatest player who ever lived, but he didn't make golf courses obsolete."

Golf didn't lengthen courses, restrict golf balls, or alter clubs because of Nicklaus, Palmer, Jones, or Nelson, and it's not likely to do so because of Woods, either. At least not yet.

"As far as the rules of golf are concerned, they change out of circumstances that arise in the field, not necessarily for one person," a USGA spokesperson said.

"The course is set up for everybody, and if one person is able to hit it 25 yards farther than the next, well, we have equipment and ball standards also, so that the equipment out there isn't going to make that much difference on how much farther you're going to hit the ball.

"It's really the individual who's going to have the impact on the game. And, as we've all seen, Tiger has had quite a major impact." ■

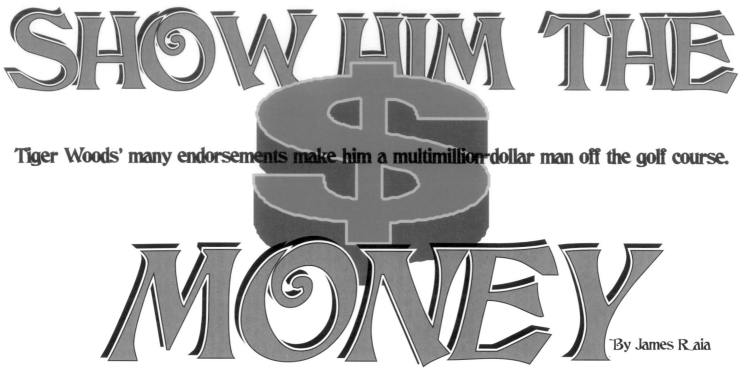

SHOW HIM THE $ MONEY

Tiger Woods' many endorsements make him a multimillion-dollar man off the golf course.

By James Raia

When Tiger Woods hits a drive off the first tee, lines up a putt on the 18th hole, or does anything anywhere else television cameras care to follow him, one thing that's hard to escape is his Nike swoosh.

It is not brightly colored, outrageously positioned, or particularly conspicuous. But Woods, with his reported $40 million Nike contract tucked away for a few rainy days, always wears shirts and hats made by the Oregon-based global sports giant. And, like all of Nike's products, Woods' apparel features the Nike logo prominently.

Within a very short time, Nike and Woods have become synonymous, just like the same company has with Chicago Bulls superstar Michael Jordan. See Tiger sink a long putt and showcase one of his thrusting uppercuts and the swoosh is there. See him smack a 330-yard drive or just walk down the fairway to his ball and there it is again.

To his credit, though, Woods chose a company with a well-known but understated insignia. And, all things considered, he isn't exactly walking down fairways with a sandwich board over his head hawking kitchen utensils or time share condos.

"It will never be the way auto racing is with sponsors on every square inch of a car and a guy talking about all those sponsors," said Bob Dorfman, a San Francisco–based sports endorsement expert with Foote, Cone and Belding. "A golfer is not going to do that, but he is going to get the logo on camera. He's not going to take his hat off (during an interview), let's put it that way. He's not going to take his shirt off, either. So, you're going to get that logo time. And that's pretty valuable (to a company)."

The champion has been, give or take a few endorsement dollars, a $100 million man. Combine Woods' recently reworked Nike deal with his other contracts with American Express, Titleist, and Rolex, among others, and it's clear that Woods is one hot commodity.

Tiger is so hot, in fact, that he is even in demand overseas. He signed a three-year, $13.5 million contract to endorse coffee and beer from Asahi, a Japanese company. Currently, Woods earns over $150 million dollars in off-course deals, endorsing products for 11 companies.

As one sports endorsement expert said, "Michael Jordan is the king of endorsements, but Tiger Woods has the potential to move into the top spot."

But beyond the bare basics of

Tiger Woods flashes a smile on May 19, 1997, after the announcement that he would be a new international spokesman for American Express.

his PGA Tour success, what makes Tiger such hot property?

Like others in the sports endorsement and advertising business, Dorfman said he looks for four specific qualities when considering an athlete to represent a client: performance (a winner on the field), personality (looks and verbal presentation), purity (accepted lifestyle) and perseverance (desire to endorse).

Dorfman cites John Stockton, the Utah Jazz guard, as a perfect example of someone who fits well into all the categories except for the last and most important one. The future NBA Hall of Fame playmaker simply does not like to endorse products.

"John is very wholesome, a great athlete, but just doesn't seem to want to do the endorsements," Dorfman said. "His time is very valuable, his private time is very cherished and he would prefer to spend that time with his family. He doesn't think the extra money or notoriety is worth it.

"You've got to find someone who wants to do endorsements, who wants to be out there and wants to give his time and effort to attach himself to a product. And pretty much on all accounts, Tiger Woods is right up there."

In addition to his desire to be a spokesperson, Woods exemplifies Dorfman's first three criteria. His performances have spoken for themselves, and his personality and lifestyle could not be better from a sponsor's perspective.

"You don't want an Albert Belle. You want someone who is open and cordial to the camera and to reporters," Dorfman explained. "And you want someone who has a little flair and carries himself well.

"You can't have a guy who's out

Tiger's Major Endorsement Deals

NIKE: Five-year deal worth $100 million
TITLEIST: Multiyear deal worth about $10 million
AMERICAN EXPRESS: Five-year deal worth $13 million
ROLEX: Five-year deal worth about $7 million

As part of a five-year deal worth $40 million, Nike's swoosh is displayed prominently on virtually all of Tiger's apparel.

drinking late at night and wraps his car around a tree. There are way too many incidents of that now, Mike Tyson being the latest. When you're dealing with millions of dollars, you just can't take that risk that something's going to blemish your product."

According to Dorfman and other industry experts, Woods epitomizes the ideal spokesperson. He's tremendously talented, and a growing segment of the population that had never before followed the sport is now interested in golf because of Tiger.

"(Tiger's) mixed ethnicity is very appealing," Dorfman said. "It kind of brings a whole new market into the world of golf. Urban basketball fans are getting into it.

"He's not just a national phenomenon, he's an international phenomenon, and that translates into even more money when you're talking about big overseas companies that can use him."

"Woods is in such demand, two of his "big-four" deals—Rolex and American Express—are with companies that at first glance don't appear to be good matches. Nike makes apparel, of course, and Titleist is perhaps the most well-known manufacturing company name in golf. But where do a credit

card company and a watch manufacturer fit in?

"By using an upscale sport like golf, it's a statement from American Express that it's going to do everything it can to make sure the AmEx name is in front of people's faces," Michael Ansell, an industry analyst at Edward Jones in St. Louis, said when the American Express deal with Woods was announced in May. "During the Masters, Tiger was wearing Nike's clothes, and you can bet it helped get the Nike 'swoosh' symbol in people's faces."

Unlike Nike and Titleist, however, American Express did not purchase the right to put its name on Woods' clothes or any of his equipment. Apparently, those details didn't matter. Kenneth Chenault, president and CEO of American Express, said Woods would help expand the company's customer base with his appearances in television commercials and by the use of his image in print advertising.

The current American Express advertising and marketing campaign slogan—"Do More"—will change with Woods in the picture. The golfer will say, or his comments will appear in print as, "I plan to do more."

Of course, Tiger Woods' status is not unique in the credit card business, as many celebrities and athletes have similar endorsements. In addition, Visa recently announced it will introduce a Jack Nicklaus credit card. Another Jack Nicklaus card, offered by Marine Midland Bank, was discontinued after a five-year run because the card didn't entice as many new cardholders as expected.

While some industry experts believe the new Nicklaus card will work, others predict it will fail in part because Nicklaus, often considered the greatest golfer in history, no longer has the same market appeal as Woods. "If they're looking for the kind of rub-off Tiger will give AmEx, it won't totally work," one analyst said. "Jack (Nicklaus) won't reposition Visa among younger consumers."

Rolex, the high-end watch manufacturer, seems an even more unlikely match for Woods, who prides himself on his support for and belief in inner-city youth golf programs. But Dorfman said he believes Rolex obviously viewed the deal with a different perspective.

"What does Tiger Woods know about Rolex? Why is he an expert? Well, he probably doesn't know much and he

Mystic Rock Charity Pro Am
May 26, 1997
Farmington, Pennsylvania

probably isn't an expert," Dorfman explained. "But again, it's kind of the cache of Tiger carrying over into the cache of the product. Maybe that's not exactly the market I saw Tiger appealing to. It does seem to be a very high-end area. However, golfers tend to be in that area.

"Look at the country clubs of the world; they are pretty much high rollers. So I think it probably makes sense for Rolex to do something like that."

While it is hard to convey the relevance of such a deal to many young people, part of his agreement with Rolex include the release of a Tiger Woods signature model watch at the low end of the Rolex line.

While Woods has become sports' second-most-sought-after endorsement figure in less than a year, he seems to be in very little danger of overexposure or of reaching a plateau of diminishing returns. He selects companies with discretion, yet his growing popularity may foster even more sponsorship deals.

But what would happen if, instead of the "mini-slump" Woods went through recently, he found himself mired in a miserable season? What would be the result if Woods had a personal dilemma like John Daly's battle with alcoholism?

"All golfers have peaks and valleys," Dorfman said. "But I think it would take a pretty long valley before a company would drop him as a spokesperson.

"What they would tend to do is just not do any more new commercials and keep him as a lower-profile athlete and highlight some of their other athletes or sign some other new players. But with Tiger Woods, that just doesn't seem likely."

After he won the Motorola Western Open in mid-July and just before he departed for the British Open, Woods was described by one media member as "Elvis reincarnated." It was also suggested to Woods that his arrival in England would be reminiscent of the reception the Beatles received when they visited the United States in 1964.

"I don't know what it's going to be like," Woods said. "And I wasn't around

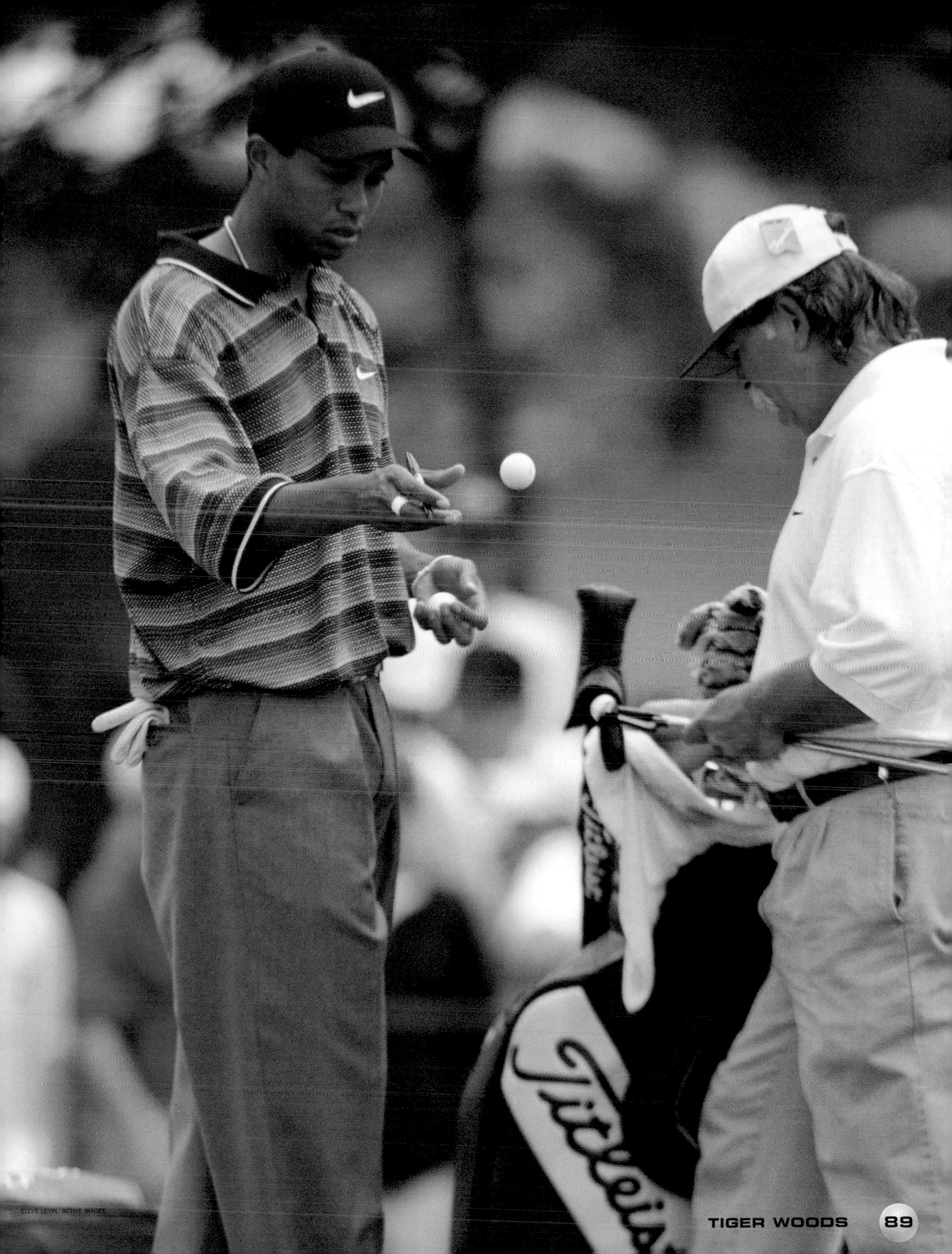

STEVE LEVIN / ACTIVE IMAGES

A young autograph seeker comes between Tiger Woods and Bryant Gumbel after an auction to benefit the Tiger Woods Foundation at New York's All-Star Cafe. Woods is a partner in the new cafe chain.

for the Beatles. But I'm not going to be what some of the people in my position have become: a prisoner of their fame."

Woods is increasingly aware of the demands for his time and those who wish to take advantage of his fame.

For instance, a lawsuit was required to stop one company from capitalizing on Woods' success. The culprit was the Franklin Mint, which was selling silver medallions that included Woods' image for $37.50 each.

Woods sued the Pennsylvania company in June, saying he had never authorized the sale of any medals bearing his likeness. The Franklin Mint claimed the company is a communications "medium" similar to a newspaper or magazine and thus is protected by the First Amendment. A district judge in Los Angeles disagreed and issued a preliminary injunction until the case goes to trial or is settled. The mint sold approximately 2,500 medals, but their delivery was stopped by the ruling.

"Tiger has entered very few endorse-ments, all with select companies, said Mark Lee, Woods' attorney, who added that the Franklin Mint medallion was a "low-end" product.

And, let's face it: Few, if any, components of Tiger Woods' ascension can be attributable to anything "low-end." ∎

By James Raia

Tiger Woods' popularity has tournament organizers scrambling to keep up with "Tigermania"

BEWARE: THERE'S A TIGER ON THE LOOSE

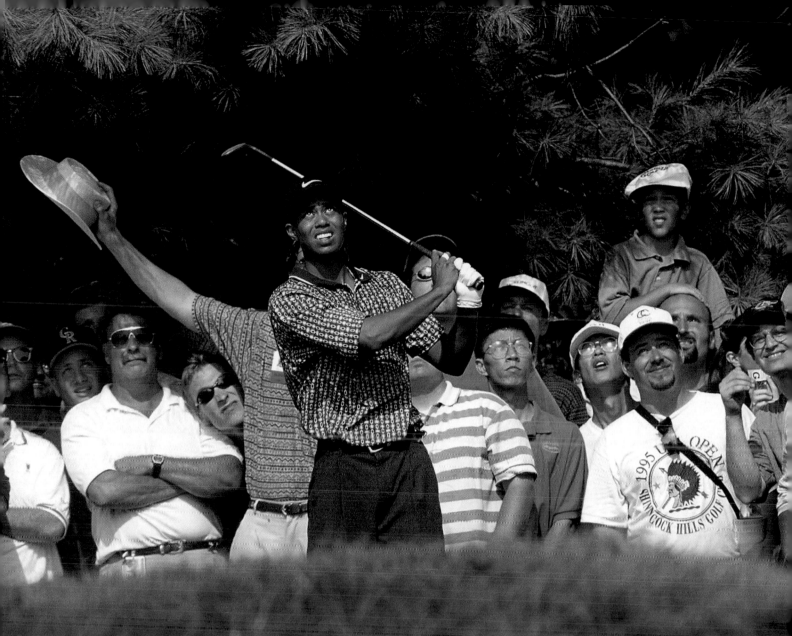

Tiger follows the flight of the ball as a crowded gallery watches his every move.

Mark Michaud has as much interest in Tiger Woods, Kevin Costner, and Bill Murray as the next golf enthusiast. But he doesn't particularly care if Woods plays well or shoots 80. And as far as he's concerned, Costner's acting skills are irrelevant and Murray's sense of humor doesn't matter.

What concerns Michaud are the growing legions who come to watch Woods, his PGA counterparts, and the celebrities play in the AT&T Pebble Beach National Pro-Am.

As golf superintendent at Pebble Beach Golf Links on the famed Monterey (California) Peninsula, Michaud oversees the course and how as many as 30,000 spectators a day will affect the course during a four-day tournament.

From parking problems to inadequate concessions and inefficient gallery ropes to environmental concerns, Michaud and other course superintendents around the country are facing an increasingly difficult task while tackling a simple fact: When Woods plays, tournament galleries drastically expand.

"Tiger has introduced golf to a new audience," said Dede Patterson, tournament director of the Buick Classic in suburban New York. "Just the thought of Tiger being in a tournament boosts ticket sales."

Patterson is a master of understatement. With Woods in the 1997 Buick Classic field, ticket sales increased 35 percent over 1996, when he wasn't in the tournament.

According to a survey and tournament analysis by The Associated Press, Woods

conservatively had a $1.13 million effect on the ten most prestigious tournaments in which he played in his first year since turning professional in August 1996. The monetary value was based on the average gallery member paying $22.50 per ticket and $24 combined on souvenirs and concessions.

The increased galleries and their increased spending habits correspond with vast increases in other Woods-related areas – television ratings, advertising revenues, marketing strategies, and equipment sales.

And, as a result, Woods was responsible for a more than $653 million infusion into the sport during his first professional year, according to The Associated Press.

And while no one's going to complain, golf course superintendents around the country

LEFT: DAVID CANNON / ALLSPORT USA; ABOVE: M. DEHOOG / GREG ABRAMOWITZ PHOTOGRAPHY

certainly aren't in any position to become complacent.

"The day after the tournament, you can pretty much tell where the (gallery) ropes were," said Michaud, who has worked at Pebble Beach for five years. "It's night and day. It's grass on one side and mud on the other."

Michaud knows of what he speaks. In addition to his tenure at one of the world's most famous courses, he's worked at two U.S. Opens as well as the Masters and Ryder Cup.

Although the Pebble Beach event has been one of the PGA Tour's most popular events since its origins as the (Bing) Crosby Clambake, the 1997 tournament reflected a nationwide trend that Woods instigated. In tournaments in which the 22-year-old phenom played, galleries increased as much as 35 percent.

But at the AT&T event in February 1999, Woods was paired with Costner, and the result could have been disastrous. While estimated crowds approaching 30,000 attended the tournament during weekend rounds, Michaud said 20,000 to 25,000 may have been following the famous twosome.

"The marshals are just under an incredible amount of pressure," said Michaud. "When you're grouping two or three huge figures like that together, galleries just concentrate on them. They (the tournament) started with the idea of spreading the bigger names throughout the course, but when they put them together, it just caused mass confusion.

"The fans buy everything starting at the first hole—all the food, all the drinks. Then they'd go to the next hole and buy everything out at that location. It dwindled as the gallery got closer to the end. But they couldn't keep the concessions full. Oh, maybe you could get a drink. But mostly, it was all gone."

Another concessions concern for tournament officials is sometimes not knowing until just prior to the tournament which players are confirmed. In Woods' instance, his appearance could double sales.

"The vendors really weren't sure if he was coming or not last year," Michaud said. "They're really pulling their hair out, saying, 'I wish I knew, because if he is coming I'll buy 100 cases of hot dogs instead of 50 cases of hot dogs.' If there's a huge difference in what they're ordering this year, it's a good bet Tiger's going to be there because

they can sell twice as much stuff. But that's a huge inventory to take on if he's scheduled to be there and then doesn't show up."

Of course, increased ticket, concessions, and souvenir sales are words that ring true for tournament directors. And while not everything about golf's increased popularity can be credited to the 1997 PGA Player of the Year, there's little doubt he was a major factor in golf's popularity boom.

"We had our best year ever in 1997," said Lou Russo, tournament director of the Pebble Beach event. "Our biggest year prior was 1995. But this year, we showed a 20 percent increase. It's hard to attribute all of it to Tiger. Golf is on an upswing, and he did play with Kevin Costner, and he did contribute to it."

Russo, a member of the PGA Tour Tournament Association, an organization of tournament directors, said his group's statistics show that the tournaments in which Woods played had gallery increases from 18 percent to 30 percent.

"We had to cut off ticket sales about a week or two before the tournament because we thought we'd be unable to serve the people," said Mac Wesson, tournament director of the Byron Nelson Classic. "We sold over $8 million in tickets and ticket packages, and we were up 20 percent in our merchandise tent and about 25 percent in food sales.

And while there aren't any apparent reasons for golf not to enjoy Woods' influence, it doesn't make superintendents' jobs any easier.

At Pebble Beach, Michaud cites horren-

Tiger Woods and Kevin Costner share tips at the 1997 AT&T Pebble Beach National Pro-Am, where the rare pairing drew a huge fan following.

dous parking problems, trampled fairways, course clean-up issues, and upset local residents as areas of increased concern. Spyglass Hill Golf Course and Poppy Hills Golf Course, the two additional layouts used at the AT&T, face similar tournament issues. But those course's problems aren't as severe since both layouts are enclosed courses with limited crowd access. Compounding the problem for Pebble Beach is that it's the only tournament course used on the final day.

"The crowds were massive, but Pebble Beach is well-suited for galleries in the first place," Michaud explained of last year's turnout. "So the tournament didn't have a huge effect on the golf course. There was a larger area to be repaired after the tournament since in that time of the year, it's usually real wet. In fact, it's our rainiest time of the year. The grass kind of gets stomped into the mud.

Tiger is never at a loss for company when he plays, as shown by the throng (inset left) that followed him up the 18th fairway to victory at the 1997 Western Open .

"But the biggest challenge we faced last year and what we're trying to improve upon, is getting the people into the tournament. The off-site parking and bus situation were just overwhelming. Cars were backed up to the highway."

New shuttle bus arrangements and other improved parking logistics may help resolve the traffic jams. A pending revamped division of major players and celebrities throughout the field should help spread the crowd.

Meanwhile, Michaud will continue to utilize creative gardening methods on the fairways and beyond the gallery rope. In fact, without the gallery even aware, they're helping restore the fairways and other grassy areas while they're trampling it throughout the week.

Prior to the tournament, Pebble Beach groundskeepers spread grass seed in various gallery areas. Because the links course is susceptible to ocean spray and seasonal torrential rains, the gallery areas are often reduced to muddy pathways by the end of tournament week.

"We take advantage of the traffic. We put down a whole bunch of seed before the galleries get on it," Michaud explained. "So afterward, it's a matter of cleaning up the garbage, and the seed then kind of comes up through the mud and the other grass that's been matted down and things kind of just grow back – in about two weeks."

While Pebble Beach didn't limit ticket sales last year, the tournament and other PGA circuit stops could face the situation that occurred last season when crowds broke through gallery ropes and followed Woods on the 72nd hole and as he marched toward victory at the Bay Hill tournament.

"We have a volunteer marshaling staff and it's spread around the course for a 20,000-person crowd," explained Michaud. "All of a sudden there's 30,000 people, and the gallery ropes aren't exactly barriers that people can't push away. But that doesn't bother us so much. It's the marshals who are under an incredible amount of pressure."

Although Woods has yet to confirm his scheduled Pebble Beach return, tournament officials are considering ways to improve last year's difficulties, including the aforementioned separation of the more popular players.

Regardless, Michaud will prepare the course the same as he's done for the past five years.

"It's intensity," he said. "You're trying to make your greens fast, but not kill them. You're trying to cut the fairways as tight as you can and make balls bounce through them into the rough. But mostly, at the AT&T we're just trying to hang on.

"Every day is a new challenge. We're using vacuums to get water out of greens. We're airifying greens right before the tournament. It's a matter of survival for our staff considering how the weather can change.

"If we can provide the players with a playable golf course, we're doing pretty good."

And the weather—as far as Michaud and anyone else knows—may be the only component of the AT&T Pebble Beach National Pro-Am that Woods can't influence. ■

Woods' incredible year leaving

By Jimmy Burch

AP/Wide World

records, opponents shattered

It is difficult to summarize Tiger Woods' historic 2000 season on the PGA Tour.

But the numbers that will stick with golf fans are in the history books and the figures that scream loudest, in the wake of Woods' playoff victory in the PGA Championship at Valhalla Golf Club in Louisville, Kentucky, are these:

3: Consecutive victories at major championships, matching Ben Hogan for the most majors won in any season by a professional golfer.

6: Consecutive victories at PGA Tour events, a streak that ended in February and included victories in his last four starts of the 1999 season. It marked the longest winning streak at tour events since Hogan won six in a row in 1948.

12: Strokes under par at the U.S. Open, the lowest score in relation to par in tournament history.

15: Consecutive rounds of par or better at major championships after posting a 75 in the opening round of the Masters.

18: Strokes under par at the PGA Championship, matching Bob May for the lowest score in relation to par in tournament history.

19: Strokes under par at the British Open, the lowest score in relation to par in tournament history.

23: Combined strokes by which Woods won the U.S. Open and British Open in consecutive starts at major championships.

24: Woods' age when he completed the career grand slam, making him the youngest player to do so.

53: Combined strokes under par in major championships, including a 49-under total during his victories.

67.6: Scoring average at this year's major championships, including a mark of 67.7 in his final 14 rounds, when Woods posted the lowest weekend scores at the Masters, then won the final three majors of the season.

How good is that?

Tom Watson, 50, deems it the best year any professional golfer has ever had.

"With the way he's played these golf courses during the major championships, you'd have to say that," said Watson, an eight-time major champion. "He has raised the bar higher than anybody has ever raised it, as far as putting distance between himself and the rest of the field. You are seeing a phenomenon that the game may never, ever see again."

Woods' dominant run through the final three majors of the season triggered chatter about a possible Grand Slam in 2001.

Nick Faldo, a six-time major champion, identified Woods as the only player on tour capable of winning a slam. He said he would not be surprised if the world's top-ranked golfer gave it a strong run in 2001. Dan Jenkins, renowned author and golf writer from Fort Worth, said he expects Woods to complete a slam at some point in his career, unless he gets hurt.

"I'm too old to get shocked by too many things," said Mark Brooks, 39, a Fort Worth resident who won the 1996 PGA. "Death and taxes will shock you. Great golf, as a rule, won't do it. But what he's done is nothing short of phenomenal."
Nick Price, 43, said he shakes his head every time he scans Woods' statistics from the past three majors.

"I played like that once in my life," Price said, referring to his six-stroke victory at the 1994 PGA. "He plays like that in every major.
It's astounding. I feel sorry for the young guys. Basically, I've had my day. Whatever I win from here on in is a bonus. But the young guys are taking a pounding from this guy. They'll have to play almost perfect golf to win a major as long as Tiger's in the field."

Statistically, Woods ranks high in all phases of the game and is regarded as the tour's ultimate power player. Yet Brooks said fans might not truly appreciate Woods' power, because he ranks second in driving distance (294.6 average), five yards behind John Daly (299.9).

"People don't understand the advantage he truly has because he doesn't hit driver on all the holes that are measured. And he doesn't max out his swing," Brooks said. "When he really cuts loose, he's hitting it 50 yards past most people, not 20. That's a huge bonus. Other guys don't have that extra gear to call on when they need it."

Watson listed other attributes as well, offering a synopsis of why Woods is atop the golfing world.

"He has better flexibility than anybody. You hear that from the trainers," Watson said. "He works out harder than anybody, hits the ball farther than anybody, putts better than anybody, chips better than anybody. He wants to be the best player who has ever lived. I think that pretty well explains it."

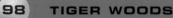

AP/Wide World

AP/Wide World

"Tiger has more athletic ability than

any golfer who has ever been great."

Tiger's father

"I think it's so important that you give kids hope. And, by being a positive role model, I think you can do that."

Tiger Woods

"**Tiger Woods transcends golf. He is magical and he is mesmerizing. He's just what our world needs right now.**"

talk show host Oprah Winfrey

"I think Tiger Woods is the best player in the history of the game. He has control of all phases of the game."

former baseball player Mike Schmidt

"This kid is the most fundamentally sound golfer I've ever seen at almost any age."

pro golf legend Jack Nicklaus

"He's a boy among men, and he's showing the men how to play."

pro golfer Tom Watson